1 0   S T E P S   T O

Be a ^ Successful Manager

Lisa Haneberg

PRESS

Alexandria, Virginia

D1416759

©October 2007 by the American Society for Training & Development.

All rights reserved. Printed in the United States of America.

11   10   09   08   07   1   2   3   4   5

No part of this publication may be reproduced, distributed, or transmitted in any form or by any means, including photocopying, recording, or other electronic or mechanical methods, without the prior written permission of the publisher, except in the case of brief quotations embodied in critical reviews and certain other noncommercial uses permitted by copyright law. For permission requests, please go to www.copyright.com, or contact Copyright Clearance Center (CCC), 222 Rosewood Drive, Danvers, MA 01923 (telephone: 978.750.8400, fax: 978.646.8600).

ASTD Press is an internationally renowned source of insightful and practical information on workplace learning and performance topics, including training basics, evaluation and return-on-investment (ROI), instructional systems development (ISD), e-learning, leadership, and career development.

Ordering information: Books published by ASTD Press can be purchased by visiting our website at store.astd.org or by calling 800.628.2783 or 703.683.8100.

Library of Congress Control Number: 2007921481
ISBN-10: 1-56286-475-0
ISBN-13: 978-1-56286-475-0

ASTD Press Editorial Staff
Director: Cat Russo
Manager, Acquisitions & Author Relations: Mark Morrow
Editorial Manager: Jacqueline Edlund-Braun
Editorial Assistant: Maureen Soyars

Copyeditor: Christine Cotting
Indexer: April Davis
Proofreader: Kris Patenaude
Interior Design and Production: UpperCase Publication Services, Ltd.
Cover Design: Renita Wade

Printed by Victor Graphics, Inc., Baltimore, Maryland, www.victorgraphics.com

Let's face it, most people spend their days in chaotic, fast-paced, time- and resource-strained organizations. Finding time for just one more project, assignment, or even learning opportunity—no matter how career enhancing or useful—is difficult to imagine. The *10 Steps* series is designed for today's busy professional who needs advice and guidance on a wide array of topics ranging from project management to people management, from business planning strategy to decision making and time management, from return-on-investment to conducting organizational surveys and questionnaires. Each book in this ASTD series promises to take its readers on a journey to basic understanding, with practical application the ultimate destination. This is truly a just-tell-me-what-to-do-now series. You will find action-driven language teamed with examples, worksheets, case studies, and tools to help you quickly implement the right steps and chart a path to your own success. The *10 Steps* series will appeal to a broad business audience from middle managers to upper-level management. Workplace learning and human resource professionals along with other professionals seeking to improve their value proposition in their organizations will find these books a great resource.

CONTENTS

P R E F A C E

I believe that great managers make great companies. As a leadership and management coach, trainer, and consultant, I've enjoyed helping managers grow and I've seen the big difference just a few small changes can make.

I've held the role of manager several times. In today's fast-moving and more complex work environments, the manager's job is becoming broader and more challenging. To achieve success, we have to be better today than we had to be in the past. Alas, not everyone is successful and many well-meaning and hard-working managers fail. I once had a friend with a heart the size of Alaska. She worked long hours and was passionate about her work. And she was fired. Why? Her department wasn't getting projects done on time and she was a time management train wreck. She promised much more than she could deliver and she let every email and phone call divert her attentions away from what was most important. Her manager talked with her several times—even offered her a coach. But she believed that if she just worked harder and longer, she could turn things around. She was wrong because she didn't spend her time on the right activities—she ignored the management fundamentals.

10 Steps to Be a Successful Manager offers a short list of the most important management fundamentals. Had my friend read this book and followed its recommendations, I believe she wouldn't have lost the job she loved. Her employees liked her very much as a person but they hoped for more from their manager. After she was fired, several people asked her manager what had taken him so long. This is a tragic story that I've seen play out many times. It's tragic because it's preventable. I hope this book helps you be more successful and productive.

Helping hard-working and well-meaning people develop their abilities to better manage their businesses is my mission and passion and I've been doing this kind of work for about 25 years. Why do I do it and love it? Because you, the successful managers, really are the engine!

Although this is a business book, I would also like you to think of it as the start of a conversation. My goal in writing *10 Steps to Be a Successful Manager* is to provoke conversations about best practices, alignment, and success. Play with the concepts in your head and modify the recommendations to fit your unique circumstances. I think it's a perfect book for informal brown-bag lunch chats and for management training sessions. To help you use this book in a group setting, I've written a companion book, *10 Steps to Be a Successful Manager Facilitator's Guide*. In the guide I offer ideas and examples for creating great conversations about management. You can use the *Facilitator's Guide* for informal meetings or regular management training sessions.

I would love to hear how you use *10 Steps to Be a Successful Manager*. Feel free to send me an email with your stories and questions. I can be reached through my website, www.lisahaneberg.com. I hope that you find *10 Steps to Be a Successful Manager* helpful to use and fun to read!

Lisa Haneberg
October 2007

INTRODUCTION

Management is the engine that drives our corporations. We require great management to ensure execution of strategies and project success, and to identify and seize new opportunities. Management is often the difference between excellent and unsatisfactory results. Being a great manager is a tough job, but it's one that offers outstanding rewards and satisfaction. Unfortunately, many managers don't perform near their potential because they let several gnarly barriers get in the way. The most common barriers to good management include

◆ **becoming a victim of circumstances.** Managers are needed to improve the organization and its results, but corporate dysfunction or immaturity can seem overwhelming. It's important to own your role in making things better and to resist becoming part of the problem.

◆ **confusing the need to manage with the need to control.** Some managers think that their job is to control people and operations. Control is a myth; you can't—and shouldn't try—to control people. The manager's job is to ensure that people are doing their very best work and using the most appropriate processes to achieve the goals of the enterprise. To do this, managers must connect to and relate with people and motivate them. Actions to control people move results in the opposite direction. Great management is a very powerful practice rooted in driven, focused service orientation and authentic relationships.

◆ **letting management become maintenance.** It's the manager's responsibility to make something happen—something that wouldn't have happened without him or her. Management should never turn into maintenance. If you're doing the same things every day and spending most of your time maintaining your piece of the business, you're not actively managing. It's easy to fall into the trap of getting comfortable with success, but managers need to resist this urge and ensure that they continue to drive performance forward.

◆ **failing to tune up and realign.** *Management A* produces *Results A*. If you want *Results B,* you can't get there using *Management A*. Great managers periodically tune up and align their practices and approaches to produce desired results. Because corporate strategies, initiatives, and goals change frequently, managers need to change, too.

Managers have great jobs. They have the opportunity to make a significant difference in their businesses and for the people with whom they lead and partner. Management is not easy and it requires you to blast through organizational politics and dysfunction. *But that's why you're here!* Embrace the challenge and triumph over the management barriers. Make this the best job you'll ever have.

Management and Leadership

Before I get into the specifics of the 10 steps, I want to address a common question: What's the difference between **management** and **leadership?** My perspective on this is likely to differ from what you've heard before or read in books about leadership. First, I don't believe that management and leadership are different positions or jobs. Many companies distinguish managers and leaders on the basis of their pecking order in the organization. That seems like nonsense to me. We see and experience leadership at all levels of the organization. Some people believe that leadership is something you do when you move beyond management—that leadership is a set of higher-level tasks and that it takes more skill to be a leader than it does to be a manager. That belief doesn't make sense either. In fact, people with all ranges of education and sophistication and at all organization levels can and do demonstrate leadership.

So let's draw the distinction. Management is a set of methods and practices—a regimen—that enables us to run a business or a piece of the business. It's a job. Leadership is not a job; *it's the way we do the job.*

Imagine four peer managers discussing the progress of a major project. The discussion itself could be considered part of management—part of the process. Having update meetings about major initiatives is a management task. Let's say that one of those managers, you, demonstrates courage and initiates a frank conversation about concerns that the others are too chicken to bring up. At your prompting, the discussion addresses important issues that need to be defined and resolved. During that display of courage—in that moment while the four of you were managing—you demonstrated leadership.

We ought to be managers all the time and to show leadership when it's needed. This is true in every job. If you're an operations manager, you ought to be a great operations manager all the time and demonstrate leadership when the situation calls for it. The same is true at all levels of the organization. Frontline workers ought to be great frontline workers all the time and lead when necessary.

The 10 steps offered in this book all fall into the category of good management practices. Along the way, I'll share examples of where and when leadership—the way you do something—will help you improve momentum and connectedness. To be most successful in a management job, you'll also demonstrate leadership.

Target Audience

10 Steps to Be a Successful Manager is for managers at all levels and with varying years of experience. Whether you're a new manager or a seasoned pro, you need to tune and align your management to make sure your hard work is producing optimal results. If you're a more experienced manager, you can use the "Tune Up and Realign" section at the end of each step to freshen up your daily regimens. As a newer manager, you'll want to follow the recommendations in a more deliberate and methodical way. Be sure to use the provided worksheets, tables, tools, figures, examples, and pointers to help you get the most from the book's recommendations. Those elements will help you envision the technique and they offer suggestions for applying the techniques to your work.

Sequence of the Steps

I am offering these 10 steps in a particular order. Whether you're a new or an experienced manager, it will work well if you follow the steps in the order I recommend. Some steps can be completed in a single meeting or planning session; other steps will take months to accomplish. You can begin working on the next step before the previous one is complete.

That said, remember that management isn't like changing a lightbulb, with specific actions coming one after the other. Management is a multifaceted position, not a single process. If you find it beneficial to skip around the book, that's fine—with this one recommendation: Always do Steps 1 and 2 in order before moving on to other steps. The work of Steps 1 and 2 is most important and most often overlooked. Underperforming managers almost always need to retune and align those two steps.

Structure of This Book

This book will help you establish or realign your managerial practices and regimens for improved results and satisfaction. Each step describes one area of action you need to develop to create a robust and healthy management practice. Here's a summary of the 10 steps:

◆ **Step 1: Clarify, Negotiate, and Commit to Your Role—**
Not all management jobs are the same, and it's important

that you understand your role as defined by your manager, employees, and peers. Discover their expectations of you and negotiate any points of disagreement or conflict.

◆ **Step 2: Understand Your Expected Results**—To manage well, you need to know what home-run performance will look like for the portion of the business you manage—in the next month, six months, the next year, and beyond. Only by clearly understanding the results your stakeholders want will you be able to manage successfully.

◆ **Step 3: Know Your Piece of the Business**—Great managers know what's working well and what areas of the business need more attention. Analyzing business metrics and improving results are important parts of any manager's job. Information is power and, with good business analysis, you can ensure that time and energy are focused on the tasks that will make the greatest difference.

◆ **Step 4: Build a Great Team**—A great team is engaged in doing its work and doesn't need excess supervision. When you tap into your employees' strengths and desires to make a contribution, you're able to direct your time and energy to proactive and meaningful endeavors.

◆ **Step 5: Choose Employees Wisely**—You have a chance to improve the strength and effectiveness of your team each time you fill an open position. The decision to hire affects you and your team for years, so it's important that you choose wisely and well.

◆ **Step 6: Define and Model Excellence**—Team members want to succeed, but they can do so only if they clearly understand what excellence looks like. Managers need to be very careful because their day-to-day actions define expectations and excellence. You need to make sure your words and actions communicate the same performance expectations.

◆ **Step 7: Plan the Work and Work the Plan—Flexibly**—Work planning is essential. There are always many more tasks to do than time available to do them. How do you ensure your team is focused on the right tasks right now? A good plan needs to be flexible because priorities change.

Know when to kill projects and shift people's energy to more important or fruitful initiatives.

◆ **Step 8: Obliterate Barriers**—If you want your team members to be productive and engaged, you need to take on the role of barrier crusher. Managers exist to facilitate the forward movement of work. Identifying and getting rid of barriers are great uses of your time and will improve results and morale.

◆ **Step 9: Proactively Manage Change and Transition**—Change is inevitable, but how people respond to change is a choice. It's important that your department be nimble in the face of change. There are many things that managers can do to promote smoother transitions when changes occur.

◆ **Step 10: Leave a Legacy of Capacity to Produce**—What mark will you leave on your department? Great managers build their teams and the organization. Determine the legacy you want to leave and then manage in a way that's consistent with your goals.

Review the 10 steps once a quarter or as your business goals change to ensure that your hard work yields the greatest benefit and job satisfaction.

Being a manager can be a blast because, as the engine of the organization, you can set the tone and pace for success. What could be more fun and rewarding than that?

Clarify, Negotiate, and Commit to Your Role

OVERVIEW

Clarifying expectations

Negotiating expectations

Aligning your management plan with expectations

Committing to your role

Please don't blow off reading this first step. I know the title may lead you to believe that its content is fundamental, but I've seen more managers languish or fail because they haven't done (or re-done) Step 1 adequately. A chasm between your and your manager's understandings of expectations can be painful and may impede your success. Let's be clear about the issues:

◆ **Assumption #1:** Most managers do a lousy job communicating and clarifying performance expectations.

◆ **Assumption #2:** Most managers do a lousy job asking their managers to define expectations.

◆ **Assumption #3:** Few managers have ongoing conversations about expectations (and I don't count performance evaluation conversations).

◆ **Assumption #4:** Without a good understanding of expectations, it's hard—even for the most talented managers—to ensure they're working on what matters most.

Managers have too many options for how they spend their time and energy. You have to make choices every day, and those choices ought to be aligned with what's expected of you. A common problem is that managers don't get beyond the job description when discussing expectations. The most important expectations are the ones that address intangibles, behaviors, and culture. In this section, I'll share several easy ways you can make sure that you, and those with whom you work, agree on expectations. Let's get into it.

POINTER

When expectations aren't comprehensive and clear, it's very difficult to make good choices about how to spend your precious time.

Clarifying Expectations

You want to know—really know—the expectations that your manager, peers, and team members have of you. Most managers don't comprehend these expectations to the depth and degree of detail that they need to be optimally successful. Expectation conversations, when they occur, often will cover a list of required or desired tasks, basic project standards (on budget, on time, at a certain level of quality), ongoing work responsibilities, and a general request to bring questions and problems to the manager.

It's nice to have that list of expectations, but you need more. You want to know what type of work environment the company wants to develop, and what ought to be your part in creating such a culture. You want to know the types of changes your manager, peers, and team members would like you to own and lead. You want to know expectations about creativity and innovation. You want to know the organization's professionalism standards, which will vary from company to company. You want to know your manager's concerns—what keeps her or him up at night. You want to know what's most important to making your employees feel great about their work and the company. You want to know the expectations of your peers regarding partnership, communication, areas of co-management, and collaboration. I could go on and on.

How do you ensure that expectations are clear? You ask. You ask your manager, peers, and team members. You ask specific questions that yield specific and helpful answers. In tool 1.1, I've offered a meaty list of questions to help you discover expectations.

I recommend taking 60 minutes or so for the first round of questioning conversations, and then allowing 20–30 minutes to update expectations. That's 60 minutes per meeting. Start with a one-on-one conversation with your manager. Next, gather several of

TOOL 1.1

Questions to Discover What People Expect from You

Topic Area	Questions to Determine Expectations
Basic job function	• How do you define quality of work? • What are your expectations regarding deadlines and communication of work status? • What does "being prepared" mean?
Decision making	• What is your expectation of me regarding making and communicating decisions? • What types of decisions would you like me to include you in making?
Work environment	• How would you describe the work environment you expect me to build and reinforce? • In what ways would you like to see the company's culture change? • What role do you believe I should play in creating that transformation? • Is there anything about the department's current culture that you think ought to change or improve?
Creativity and innovation	• What does it mean to "be creative"? • How important are creativity and innovation, and what are your expectations of me regarding them? • In what ways would you like me and my group to generate new ideas and improve results?
Team development and productivity	• Will you describe for me your vision of how a well-functioning team looks and feels? • What expectations do you have regarding team development and productivity? • What are your expectations regarding the way I will manage and correct poor performance?

continued on next page

STEP 1

Topic Area	Questions to Determine Expectations
	• How much time do you think I ought to spend coaching others?
Communication	• What does "effective communication" look like to you? • What are your expectations of me regarding communication? • What do you expect of me regarding attending and conducting meetings?
Growth and development	• Everyone needs to continue to grow. In what two ways would you most like to see me grow and develop over the next year?
Results orientation	• What does it mean to be "results oriented"? • What are your expectations of me regarding getting results and being results oriented?
Partnership	• How important are partnership and collaboration? • What are your expectations of me regarding our level of partnership and collaboration? • In what ways would you like to see partnership and collaboration improve?
Ethics and role modeling	• What does it mean to "represent the company well"? • What are your expectations for how managers will conduct themselves and represent the company?

your peers as a group and ask the questions. (This makes for a very interesting conversation because while you're clarifying what they expect of you, you also reinforce your expectations of them—a win–win). Finally, ask the questions of your team members, first in a group meeting and then on a one-to-one basis as part of your regular conversations with each person. This sounds like a lot of meetings, but the time will be well spent and you only have to do it occasionally. Hey, while you're at it, do this with your spouse or significant other! The questions for your partner aren't included here, but you can use the questions in tool 1.1 as a starting point for the conversation. Add questions about topics on which you're most curious or unclear.

The questions in tool 1.1 are great! Can you honestly say you know your manager's, peers', and team members' answers to the questions right now? Getting through all the questions will take some time, but it's worth the effort—I promise you. Do the process, as I described above, at least annually—or twice a year if your job or focus changes a lot. In addition, don't miss any chances to calibrate your understanding of expectations throughout the year. Things change and memories fail. There are many opportunities to clarify expectations, and doing so is important because our bosses and peers forget what they said last week—never mind six months ago. I can't count the number of times I've said something like this to my manager, just to ensure that we're on the same page:

> Jane, I assume you want me to focus on creating a consistent process for evaluating and changing our products, right? Great. To that end, I'm concerned about adding a bunch of ad hoc tactical meetings. My assumption is that you expect me to help the organization resist knee-jerk reactions and changes. Is that correct?

POINTER

If you really want to know what your manager, peers, and team members expect, move beyond questions about specific projects and go deeper to understand the *type* of manager they hope you will be.

That's just an example, but you get the idea. Nothing can sweep us off target faster than a bad idea (or a knee-jerk idea) well communicated in a staff meeting. How many times have you seen this happen? There's a plan in place, but someone mentions an idea at a staff meeting and everyone forgets the plan ever existed! You'll see in Step 7 that I don't recommend being too rigid when adhering to plans—sometimes things must change. That said, many managers let what's urgent determine their path, and that may not be the best long-term approach. When this happens to you, help your manager remember the hopes and expectations you agreed to previously, and point out how abandoning that path will affect the department. Managers often have one set of expectations in their minds and another set that's reinforced by their actions. Instead of letting that haze of confusion reduce your effectiveness and gunk up your focus, be proactive in having conversations that bring the head and hand expectations together.

Negotiating Expectations

Are you all on drugs? That question may come to mind after you collect everyone's expectations and add them up. You can't do it all, and you can't stuff 200 pounds into a 100-pound bag. But we try,

POINTER

Expectations for All Managers

Along with the expectations that address your specific function, industry, and company, I think that these expectations apply to most all management positions:

- *Managers are expected to be accountable and take ownership.* To achieve results, you need to own whatever must be accomplished. This ownership and accountability drive proactivity and help stave off procrastination.
- *Managers are expected to make a positive contribution to the business.* Your job is to think creatively and proactively, and to take initiative to improve your team's performance. Knowing this reinforces the concept that it's *not* a manager's job to maintain or oversee what would otherwise happen on its own. You will know and analyze the piece of the business you've been asked to run.
- *Managers should be outstanding role models* because they influence the culture and tone of the business. You need to represent the best of what you seek in others. It's not OK for managers to be unprofessional or model undesirable behaviors. You'll enjoy more success as a manager if you take your role as a professional seriously and recognize that your team members and peers are watching and emulating you when they decide how to respond to situations.
- *Managers need to get results.* Managers who believe that it's their job to execute work and deliver results are more likely to choose results-oriented actions and responses. They also are more apt to value productivity measurements and process improvements as tools for monitoring, managing, and enhancing results.

don't we? And, remember, you haven't yet added project-specific goals and work products to your planning plate—that's Step 2.

Your work so far has yielded basic expectations, and likely far too many of them. It's clear that some paring down has to happen. It's time to negotiate a more practical and realistic set of expectations. Let's consider some scenarios in which expectations might be negotiated or modified:

◆ You've been asked to spend more time coaching and developing people. Your peers and team members also requested more one-on-one time with you, but your meeting schedule already soaks up much of your day.

- *Management is both a social function and a business function.* With every meeting and every conversation in which you participate, you have the opportunity to either add to or detract from the quality of the relationship. Managers need the support and cooperation of those with whom they work. Operating in isolation won't yield success. Flexible and nimble teams are more successful. You need to have your finger on the pulse of the company and know when changes in approach make sense. Understanding this expectation keeps you more open to exploring options and creative solutions. You'll be less likely to draw comfort from the status quo.
- *Being a manager is an important role.* Managers should want to spend most of their time managing and facilitating the work of others. Managers who don't believe the job is interesting and desirable aren't likely to serve themselves or the organization well. Love the work or get out.
- *Success as a manager means delivering results and managing people for optimal productivity and satisfaction.* To be truly effective you must reframe your definition of success based on accomplishment and your ability to build the organization's capacity to produce.
- *Managers are responsive to other people's ideas and concerns.* Being defensive or combative doesn't reflect favorably on any manager. Being open and flexible makes you seem more intelligent and talented. If you always need to prove that you're right, you'll undermine relationships with everyone around you.
- *Managers must know when to lead—and do so.* This may demand courage and might mean taking a risk. Moments of leadership inspire and align people and the organization.

◆ You've been asked to create a culture of creativity and innovation—and to up the percentage of billable hours. These seem to be conflicting expectations.

◆ You're a working manager. Over 50 percent of your time is dedicated to nonmanagerial projects and tasks—*doing* versus *managing*. But your manager, peers, and team members are looking for you to manage at the same level as full-time managers in the organization. This seems neither fair nor realistic.

◆ Your manager wants you to better represent the company with your employees. Your employees want you to better represent their needs and concerns to the company. How can you satisfy both parties?

◆ Everyone acknowledges that the work culture needs to change, and your department needs to shift the way it does business. It seems, however, that your manager and peers expect this to happen overnight. A lot of changes need to occur to get from point A to point B.

Conflicting and unrealistic expectations are common, and it's your job to recognize and negotiate them so you can be successful. Sometimes you don't have the time or skills to accomplish all requests, and sometimes you need to get a better understanding of what the expectations mean. For example, managers do need to represent both the company and the needs of their employees. They're the lens that helps senior management see things from the frontline employee's perspective and helps the frontline employee see things through the senior manager's eyes.

When I was a manager, I revisited expectations quarterly and then made sure that actions and words were clarified and aligned. Doing that was important to me because I wanted to stay focused. Differences between intention and action can cause scope creep and loss of impact.

You may find your list of expectations inspiring and challenging, and you may feel you don't need to negotiate them. Great! Just don't make the mistake of filing the notes from your expectation-discovery conversations in a folder and revisiting them in six months. You'll generate the best results when your thoughts, actions, and measures are aligned with your goals. For expectations to influence your management regimen, you need to translate them into aligned daily actions.

Aligning Your Management Plan with Expectations

How should expectations shape your daily management practices? Expectations ought to form the foundation for how you manage— they create the filters through which you make choices about how to spend your precious time. Once you agree to a set of expecta- tions, it becomes your general managerial goal—or the way in which you'll manage. Let's say that you're expected to build a strong and collaborative team environment. That expectation should affect how you plan and facilitate team meetings, divvy as- signments, manage projects, and measure success. You might even change the physical layout of the office and which communication tools you use to connect remote team members. If you're being held accountable for building a strong and collaborative team, you'll want to ensure that the team environment promotes and reinforces collaboration and connection, that team members are trained to collaborate, and that you build a culture of trust and openness. The management practices that build a strong and collaborative team look wildly different from the practices that build a highly individ- ualized and compliant team.

I've used a tool called the Management Filter for many years. The filter helps managers understand expectations in a way that's con- crete and actionable. Creating a Management Filter that supports your general managerial goals—the expectations you have agreed to own—is easy. Start with a form such as worksheet 1.1. Think about how each expectation shows up in various aspects of your work. Take a look at example 1.1 to see how the filter works using the common expectations for managers that I presented earlier in this step.

WORKSHEET 1.1

The Management Filter

Instructions: In the first column, list expectations (the results *you* are expected to produce, not what you expect of others). In column two, translate each expectation into a question. For example, if you're expected to build collaboration, column two might read, "To what degree does taking this action or making this decision increase team member collaboration?" You want to translate the expectation into a question that will help you determine how well your actions and decisions support the achievement of the expectation. When you have columns one and two filled in, you can use the filter. That is, you assess potential actions and decisions for alignment with expectations by assessing whether each one supports your intentions. Circle **LOW, MEDIUM,** or **HIGH** to indicate how well the action or decision supports your expectation. For example, if you want to improve collaboration and you have decided to begin weekly collaboration meetings, you would rate alignment as HIGH.

Expectation	Filter Question: To what degree does taking this action or making this decision...	Level of Support for This Expectation
		LOW MEDIUM HIGH
		LOW MEDIUM HIGH
		LOW MEDIUM HIGH

	LOW MEDIUM HIGH
	LOW MEDIUM HIGH
	LOW MEDIUM HIGH
	LOW MEDIUM HIGH
	LOW MEDIUM HIGH
	LOW MEDIUM HIGH
	LOW MEDIUM HIGH
	LOW MEDIUM HIGH

EXAMPLE 1.1

Management Filter: Basic Management Expectations

Expectation	Filter Question: To what degree does taking this action or making this decision...	Level of Support for This Expectation		
Accountability and ownership	demonstrate my ownership and acknowledge the results for which I am accountable?	LOW	MEDIUM	HIGH
Make a positive contribution	make a positive difference to the business, the work culture, or my function?	LOW	MEDIUM	HIGH
Role model	present a positive and professional image of which I and the company can be proud?	LOW	MEDIUM	HIGH
Results orientation	demonstrate my focus and attention on producing results?	LOW	MEDIUM	HIGH
Master conversationalist and relationship builder	build the quality of dialogue and build productive relationships?	LOW	MEDIUM	HIGH
Focus on great management	show my commitment and dedication to solid management of my function and team?	LOW	MEDIUM	HIGH

	LOW	MEDIUM	HIGH
Focus on accomplishment and organizational capacity	help build our results, and build the team's and the organization's capacity to deliver results in the future? To what degree does doing this make things better for today and tomorrow?		
Inclusive and responsive	benefit from the ideas, concerns, and input of others? To what degree am I showing that I care about and will consider other perspectives and points of view?		
Well-executed moments of leadership	demonstrate leadership? Am I stepping up to make a significant difference?		

If we imagine creating a filter for the expectation of building strong and collaborative teams, it ought to prompt you to think about your actions and decisions relative to that expectation. Each day and week, you can use the filter to make better choices about how you use your time. For example, facilitating collaborative planning sessions or ideas-generating meetings should rank pretty high in importance. It would also be crucial to align measures and rewards to reinforce collaboration and strong relationships. It's important to ask yourself what you can do today that will improve team strength and collaboration. This is a broad question, but the filter helps you consider several possible ways that you can have an impact, including

◆ how the work environment looks and feels

◆ how meetings are scheduled, planned, and facilitated

◆ how you make and communicate decisions

◆ how roles are structured

◆ how communication and problem-identification processes operate

◆ how changes are decided, announced, and implemented

◆ how projects are planned, structured, and implemented

◆ how individuals and teams are measured and reinforced

◆ how roles interrelate

◆ how diversity and disagreement are handled

◆ how well you focus on the work that matters most

◆ how you define, communicate, and manage the expectations you have for your staff and peers

◆ how systems are structured.

POINTER

I love the Management Filter! Use it to make sure your actions are aligned with your intentions.

The Management Filter is a great tool that can help you act in concert with expectations. I've also used this filter to help management teams collectively ensure their actions and decisions are aligned with their common organizational goals. It's simple but very powerful. You'll also find this filter works with your team.

Now it's your turn. Fill out worksheet 1.1, using the instructions included there, to reflect the expectations your manager, peers, and team members have for you.

Committing to Your Role

This may seem surprising to you, but I've met many managers who've failed to commit to their role. Instead of owning the job, they become victims of their work. This is an area I focus on a lot when interviewing management candidates—to what degree have they owned past roles, and to what degree have they become victims of their work? It's disappointing how many smart professionals allow themselves to become job victims. If management candidates haven't owned their role, I don't recommend them.

When we focus on something, we get more of it. If your mind and heart are focused on how tough your job is and how your situation is no-win, then that's what you'll get more of—the things you don't want! It's easier to be weak and abdicate responsibility, but who wants to do that? My guess is that you have become a manager because you want to make a positive difference. You want to leave your company and team in better shape than when you started your job. Committing to your role is a big and important step.

What does it mean to commit? When we make a commitment, we're making a contract. If you never commit to managing on the basis of agreed expectations, you don't have the burden of following through. Life is easier when things remain fuzzy and ill defined. But easy is not always good. We want to feel the burden of responsibility—it's a powerful emotion that will drive us to do our best work.

We need to commit—we ought to want to commit—to our roles. When we commit, we sign up for an adventure and say, Let's go for it! Sure, it can be scary or intimidating, but all great endeavors challenge us to be our best. For maximum impact, you should commit publicly to your manager, peers, and team members. It might go like this:

Thanks for sharing your expectations of me. I have put them all together and thought about how these expectations might look and feel in action. Now that I've done that, I am ready to commit to the following basic managerial goals for the next year: *[insert your goals here]*. Is this consistent with your thoughts and hopes? *[Get responses.]* I will be asking for your cooperation, support, and coaching along the way. Thanks for your input thus far, and I welcome any ideas or comments you have.

Making the commitment public is powerful for three reasons. First, sharing goals helps us articulate and clarify what we want to accomplish. Second, when we share our intentions with others, we enhance our degree of resolve and commitment. Third, when we verbally commit to an action or a goal, we receive greater support and cooperation from those who've witnessed that commitment.

Tune Up and Realign Strategy for Step 1

◆ Have you been in your role for a while? Take the time to use the questions in tool 1.1—or those that you think are most important—and ask your boss and your team to share their expectations over two 20-minute conversations. If you have the time, ask several peers, too. You'll likely learn a few new things that haven't been high on your list of priorities.

◆ Based on what you learn from those conversations, create a quick Management Filter using the format in worksheet 1.1.

◆ Test your actions and decisions during the next week to ensure that you're in tune with expectations.

N O T E S

_____

_____

_____

_____

_____

_____

_____

_____

_____

_____

_____

_____

_____

_____

_____

_____

_____

_____

_____

_____

_____

_____

_____

_____

_____

Understand Your Expected Results

OVERVIEW

Defining results

Defining the grand-slam home run

Communicating targets

Celebrating grand slams

Step 1 enabled you to discover the basic expectations for how your manager, peers, and team members want you to manage. These expectations become your general management goals—*how* you will do your job. Step 2 focuses on the *what*. What do you and your team need to accomplish over the next year, six months, month, and week?

I've worked with several managers who struggled with this step. They let the daily urgent issues fill up their days. They defined success as working hard. Most of the managers I've known who have failed worked very hard. But hard work and success aren't always highly correlated.

I know there are times that feel like the daily fires are demanding your attention, but managers are *not* just a cog in the wheel. You're the engines and you set the pace of the work, workplace, and results. The last thing we want to do is sit back and let the daily to-dos flood our brains and bodies from morning until evening.

Step 2 is important because there are far too many good things to do in any given day. We need to focus on the few great things that will move work forward and create an agreement with our managers about what's most important. We want to produce great results, to contribute to the success of our organizations. We want to feel successful and we want our teams to win and thrive. We want to produce outstanding work—products and services that make us proud. To do all of that, we need to understand which results matter most.

What Are Results?

Results is a funny word, and we throw it around to mean a lot of different things. Are you results oriented? How would you know results orientation if you saw it? By definition, a *result* is an effect or outcome. Sounds simple enough, but many aspects of our work

POINTER

Change your definition of a result—raise the hurdle! Anyone can produce results, but only the best managers can produce results that make a big difference.

don't fit into neat outcome packages. If you manage a manufacturing line, part of your measures of success will be pretty straightforward—numbers of widgets produced at X quality and cost and in X number of days. But what if you manage the human resources department or the product development group? You need to be very careful about how you define a result because when you focus on these goals, you'll get more performance in these areas.

For example, let's imagine that you manage the HR department. What's a likely result for the HR team? Throughout the years, I've seen HR departments measure the following elements:

- ◆ turnover—positive and negative
- ◆ rates of retention
- ◆ time to hire
- ◆ percent of positions filled
- ◆ benefit enrollments
- ◆ paperwork compliance
- ◆ percent of employees attending orientation

- audit scores
- number of lawsuits or claims
- completion of the employee handbooks
- performance appraisals completed
- training class registrations.

Which of those indicators—if any—are results? Based on the definition of a result as an outcome, all of those could be results. But should they be considered as such? If yes, a company could have a very results-oriented HR department filled with individuals focused on some of the wrong things! And if we use those measures to set goals, determine performance evaluation ratings, and adjust pay, we'll create a big, hairy system that's reinforcing the wrong performance expectations.

Here's my point. There are far too many things that *could* be considered results. And the most important work might be hard to define in terms of results. Using the HR example, don't we want talented people to love the company environment, feel energized, and stay with the company? Isn't that pretty important? None of the measures listed above would tell you if talented people were engaged or how long they stayed with the company.

Stop thinking about being results oriented—anyone can produce results—and stop using results orientation as some sort of yardstick for managerial success. It's meaningless. The manager's job is to produce the right kind of results and results that have an additive effect on the organization—results that leave the organization in better shape with each successive result. I like the metaphor of a grand-slam home run to frame the right kind of results a manager is seeking.

Defining the Grand-Slam Home Run

Grand-slam home run is a term from baseball. When a batter hits the ball out of the park (and not in foul territory), it's called a home run. The batter runs the bases and scores a run, or one point. If there are any players already on a base (first, second, and/or third base), they also get to run to home plate and score a point. When a batter hits a home run and there are players on all three bases, this is called a grand-slam home run because it results in the highest possible number of points: four runs or four points. The grand-slam home run makes the most out of the team's efforts and has an added benefit of creating a feeling of success throughout the organization.

I like using the grand-slam home run as a benchmark for managerial results because everything we do ought to have a positive and additive effect on our teams, peers, and the organization. If you're going to do something, make it a grand slam! If we're going to engage people in meaningful work, let's do work that makes everyone feel like a winner.

Sounds nice, I know, but let's take this metaphor and put it into action. To do that, start by having a conversation with your manager. Ask your manager to clarify the key results you and your team need to produce over the next year. For each key result, ask him or her what a grand-slam home run would look like. For example, if a key result is to successfully implement the new accounting system within budget by August 1, a grand-slam home run might be to

◆ complete the implementation by July 1, before the busy season

◆ involve the accounting team in the project such that ownership and acceptance are high

◆ implement the project while improving accountant computer skills so they can better use the new system's features

◆ develop robust contingency plans to cover any potential project setbacks

◆ reduce the costs spent on the project—harness the creativity of the group to find the best way to transition to the new system.

There's getting a project done, and then there's doing a project in such a way that many other aspects of the work are improved as well—that's great planning and management. As a driven and talented manager, you want to know what excellence looks like. Actually, you need to know because you must be able to define excellence for your team (Step 6).

Some of you might be thinking that talking about grand slams will set you up for failure because the boss will then expect nothing but grand slams from you and your team. Sure, I'll admit that openly discussing grand slams changes expectations—yours and your boss's. But that's a good thing. My goal with this step is to help set you and your team up to make amazing contributions. Identifying what *great* looks like is an important part of this. Think about the earlier example. If you don't identify what a grand slam looks like, what are the chances that you'll go for that higher level of performance? The chances are low because we get what we focus on.

STEP 2

POINTER

Define and strive for the grand-slam home run to have the deepest and broadest positive impact on the organization.

Take some time to go over your major projects and tasks with your manager, and define what a grand-slam home run would look like for each and every one. After you discuss the major deliverables with your boss, create a spreadsheet or table that looks something like example 2.1. List the goals you've settled on, and then define each one in grand-slam terms. Explain what aspects make it a grand slam.

What a cool document! Once you've typed this up, share it with your manager, confirm that you interpreted his or her input correctly, and get agreement on your deliverables and which are most important. Hold the spreadsheet in your hand and breathe a sigh of relief—many managers haven't a clue what they're supposed to do—but you do know. It feels great to know, in depth, the results that you should produce for the organization. Remember that Step 1 told you *how* you ought to manage. Now you've got a chart of deliverables that tells you *what* to do. I love clarity.

One caveat about all this clarity—things change. You'll want to update your chart monthly or as needed. It's important that it

EXAMPLE 2.1

Sample Grand-Slam Home Run Goals

Goal	What a Grand Slam Looks Like	Why This Is a Grand Slam
Implement new booking engine by end of second quarter, within budget	Booking engine is implemented and welcomed by the staff. We've created contingency plans and ensured everyone is trained and feels comfortable with the new system before the switch is flipped. We've used this opportunity to train back-up staff. We've created positive momentum and excitement for the change that will fuel and support the next phases of booking development.	We're making a major change while reducing risk and increasing people's comfort and competence with the new system. We're taking the time and initiative to get people involved and active with the new system. We're building the team's energy for and ability to transition.
Cross-train staff by end of year, without going over budget	We use the cross-training as a way to better get to know people's strengths and career goals. Create a cross-training plan that builds collaboration and cooperation among people in different jobs. Build a plan that can account for absences and vacations so that the cross-training doesn't get set aside if someone is away. Cross-train at least two people for each position.	The plan is robust and more likely to be implemented as intended. Most cross-training plans get set aside because they don't account for changes. The plan also reinforces our need to create better relationships and understand people's strengths and career interests.
Develop and implement a product development review process by July 31	Take the time to talk to key stakeholders before creating the process. Create a process that will be widely supported by key stakeholders, one that respects everyone's precious time. The process should include practices that continue the review in the event that some participants are out of town. The process ought to be inclusive while not getting out of hand in terms of the number of people sitting in meetings. Create a process to ensure that product managers collect and communicate key analyses and metrics before the review meetings occur.	Creating the project with these considerations will ensure that people are prepared to participate and that decisions can be made in a timely manner. This approach also will support our goals to use time wisely and be inclusive.

POINTER

Your manager expects the grand slam, whether you define what that looks like or not.

always contains the current version of grand-slam home runs and what's most important.

This process defines extraordinary results although it does put some pressure on you and your team to perform at a higher level—but it's all good. Would you like to know that you need to climb to the summit of Mount Rainier or would you prefer to remain oblivious to that expectation and fool around in the foothills all year long? If you know the summit is your target, you'll prepare, train, and approach the mountain ready for the long journey. Here's an important point—whether you have the grand-slam conversation with your manager or whether you don't: the grand slam is already in his or her mind. Your manager wants you and your team to reach the summit. She or he wants double benefits and contingency thinking. If you don't take the time to define grand slams, you'll miss out on an opportunity to align with your manager's hopes for you and your department.

Communicating Targets

Your lovely list of deliverables and grand-slam goals is a great communication tool. Start with your peers and get their input. You might find that they'd like you and your manager to consider a few alterations to the plan. Make the changes and then share the list with your team. Members of the team need to know what you've been asked to accomplish. The more they know, the better able they'll be to focus on what matters most and to deflect distractions. Also, seeing the game plan is exciting, and sharing it with them is the first step to figuring out how to get it all done.

I need to take a quick diversion here to write about **empowerment** (a term that I hate but a concept that's vital to your managerial success). You want to involve your employees in planning and decision making as much as possible, and it's important that you're clear about their ability to influence outcomes—both when they can and when they can't. Most teams don't influence the basic goals for the department—that's usually a negotiation between a senior manager and the department manager. The team ought to be able to influence how the work is planned and implemented. You also should get and consider the team's input when thinking about departmental changes (unless you're unable to do that). Employees sometimes fear that their managers will agree to take on too much—that they won't have the courage or resolve to tell a senior manager that she or he can't have it all. Their fears are justified because I've seen many managers agree to projects that their teams had no capacity to take on and implement successfully. When you meet with your manager to determine the deliverables, negotiate the list to make sure it's realistic. You don't want to elicit groans and the rolling back of eyeballs when you present the department deliverables to your team. If you have questions about whether something can get done in the manner or within the time desired, let your manager know you'll discuss the project with your team. Then get members' input and go back to your manager with a realistic recommendation.

Your level of inclusion also should reflect the maturity of your team and the company culture. If you have a strong and open environment, ask your manager to have the initial conversation about deliverables with you and your team. Create your grand-slam spreadsheet together. All of this empowers your team members—involving them in decisions and planning, and being clear and honest in defining the matters they can and can't influence.

Celebrating Grand Slams!

If you take the time to define what extraordinary performance looks like, it's very important to celebrate success when you and your team achieve it. This shouldn't be an all-or-nothing issue. If you accomplish the basic project or initiative goals, *any* grand-slam elements achieved are cause for celebration. When you celebrate, make sure people know why their extra efforts are extraordinary. Be specific. What are the lasting effects? How will future changes benefit from their hard work? How have they made a mark on results and on the organization? You get more of the performance on which you focus—when you celebrate extraordinary efforts, you get more. Yippee! Shoot for the moon and enjoy the journey. By setting grand-slam home run goals, and then using those goals to guide the team, you'll make a big difference in your team's results and success.

Tune Up and Realign Strategy for Step 2

◆ Take 30 minutes today and look at the two or three most important projects or goals you have for the month or year.

◆ Define what a grand slam looks like—and be sure to get your team's input on that.

◆ Start talking with your team about each goal with the added elements in mind.

◆ Talk about the difference the team could make if it achieved a grand slam.

◆ Celebrate—in a big way—when you hit your grand-slam goals.

Know Your Piece of the Business

OVERVIEW

Selecting measurements

Creating measurement practices

Managing on the basis of your metrics

Information is power. Good information enables you to make better decisions. Better decisions lead to improved results. Do you know how well your team is performing? What measures do you look at on a daily, weekly, or monthly basis?

Here's a true story that's a fine example of why it's important to do the right kind of good analysis. I was working with a medium-size company, a service firm. Its results were poor, with losses over the previous three years, and there was a real danger of failure. The management team was filled with smart, hard-working, and well-intentioned professionals. The company offered several service products through a variety of channels—direct to the consumer, through resellers, and through wholesale partnerships. The management team had product development, sales, and marketing strategies and activities to address each of those business channels. To increase sales, the company was working with its partners to market more products. The management team generally looked at the sales by channel, but not at the costs by channel; when it did look at the costs, a whole new picture emerged. This company offered premium sales commissions to several key partners. It also committed to spending marketing and sales dollars to help those partners market the products to their customers. When the firm looked at the revenue from and costs of those wholesale partnerships, it found that with some partnerships it was losing money on each sale! Up to that point, management's turnaround strategies had focused on improving the amount of business generated through those partnerships—an approach that would have led to further losses and perhaps to the company's failure. And the team discovered a second place where its metrics were lacking. It calculated product margins based on top-line costs, but didn't factor in salary and administration costs per product. When managers looked at each product and accounted for all costs, they found that a few products would never offer an acceptable return. This management team was looking at the wrong measures and making poor business decisions as a result. Once managers began studying the complete margin and cost profiles by channel and by product, they were able to make adjustments that improved their results.

If you look at the right data, you can make good decisions and ensure your success. If your metrics don't tell the whole or right story of what's going on in your business, you could be headed for failure without even knowing it.

Selecting Measurements

As that example showed, we need to measure department performance, and we need to select the right measures. Remember the HR department example from Step 2? Would measuring the time it takes to fill open positions be a good indicator of success? Not likely. If the department fills positions quickly, but with people who are not the right match for jobs, that's no success. In fact, the company probably would lose money by focusing on speed because turnover and employee replacement costs are very high. It's much cheaper to take more time and care to get the right person for each open position.

Managers should know what's going on in their departments. The ability to measure and analyze business results is a core management skill—for managers at all levels. Measures can offer early warning signs that a project is going off track or that barriers are getting in the way of results. Picking the right measures takes a bit of work, but don't let metrics and analysis intimidate you. Once you get on a regular routine for looking at the business from an analytical perspective, you'll learn to be much more comfortable working with the data.

STEP 3

Do you know what you should be measuring? Measurement takes time and energy, so you don't want to measure for measurement's sake alone. It's important to be choosy about the metrics you maintain so that the analysis doesn't take over as a major drain on resources. Here are a few questions that will help you determine the best metrics:

- What's the most important contribution that you and your team can make to the business? How can you measure performance of that contribution?
- If things are going well, how do you know why they're going well? If things are going poorly, how will you know what's happening?
- Look at the measures you have in place today. Do they focus on what matters most?
- Referring to Step 2, how will you know if you and your team are achieving excellence?
- How would your peers measure your success?
- How would your customers measure success?

> **POINTER**
>
> Measurement takes time and energy. Make sure you're measuring the right business indicators.

When selecting metrics, think about what excellence looks like to your internal and external customers. Look at customer survey data or letters and comments to get a feel for what's most important to customers. Take some time to create the right measures— just a few—that will tell you what you need to know about your part of the business.

I've known several managers who looked at the reports that the accounting department generated, but never moved beyond those. Such reports often include monthly expense summaries, budgets, forecasts, and company or division profit-and-loss statistics. The basic monthly reports may be helpful for understanding your spending, but they're not likely to give you an indication about how well your department is running. This is an area of management that requires some initiative and independence. Your accounting department might be perfectly happy if you review its monthly reports and turn in budgets and forecasts on time. But *you* should not be happy with that level of analysis because it won't tell you what you need to know about how well your department is performing relative to the results you're expected to produce (Step 2).

To identify your most important metrics, try working through Worksheet 3.1 with your team. I recommend that you book a 60-minute team meeting and email the worksheet questions to your team members a couple days before the meeting. Also, make a copy of the examples in this step (the service company and the HR example) and hand those out to people as a pre-reading assignment. You want people to challenge the current metrics if they deserve to be challenged. As a team, you don't want to get caught unaware of what's really happening because you're looking at the wrong information. Have some fun with this conversation, and make sure you hear everyone's ideas—the quiet ones often say the wisest things! You also may want to invite your manager and any peers who work closely with your team.

> **POINTER**
> Go beyond the reports that come from accounting because they may not tell you how well your department is operating.

The worksheet questions will help you have a productive team meeting about metrics. Go into the meeting open to the possibility that you ought to be measuring performance indicators that you're not currently tracking—and perhaps ones that you have no idea how to measure. After you and your team agree on the measures,

WORKSHEET 3.1

Determining Metrics

Instructions: Answer these questions as a group at your next team meeting. Use the answers to help you narrow and focus your list of the metrics to track regularly.

1. Why does this team exist? In what ways is it expected to contribute to the company?

2. What are our current department metrics, and what is our current level of performance on these metrics?

3. Do these measures indicate how well our department is performing against the key areas to which the company expects us to contribute?

4. If we were to ask our key internal or external customers, would they think these metrics were most important? If not, what indicators would our customers advocate we measure?

5. Can we do well on these metrics and produce poor results? If so, why?

6. If we could look at only two indicators to determine the team's results, what would those two indicators be? What's the best way to measure those indicators? At what frequency should we measure and review them? Who should own the collecting and communicating of data? How are we performing against these metrics today—do we know?*

7. How should we move forward?

*If the answer is "no," get that done very rapidly and have another quick review meeting with the team.

share them with your manager and peers to get their support and agreement.

Creating Measurement Practices

Selecting the right measures gets you and your team halfway there in terms of knowing your part of the business. In the opening example, my client realized that the management team was looking at the wrong financial indicators. That was a breakthrough. What came next transformed the business (a bigger breakthrough). Managers started talking about the right measures at every meeting, and they adopted decision-making practices based on new performance standards. For example, they created a filter for determining whether wholesale deals met the minimum margins and began rejecting proposals that failed to bring in the bottom-line dollars. This may seem perfectly logical, but they had been much more focused on revenue generation, or just top-line numbers, before they changed their metrics. Together, members of this management team created a set of practices that enabled them to review and make decisions based on the right metrics.

You need to do the same thing. Figure out the right indicators and measurement standards for your area, and then create a practice for how those metrics are measured, updated, and communicated. Be as transparent as possible because information is power, and the more your team members are aware of what's working and what's not, the more proactive they will be in achieving team success.

POINTER

When you have regular weekly or monthly conversations about key (that is, the right) metrics, you and your team can better focus and produce your best results.

Returning to our HR department example, imagine what would happen if, at meetings and planning sessions, the HR team tracked the time between when a position opens and when a new person is hired. If the team members focus on this metric and talk about it, they'll align their actions, as a team, to improving the speed of the recruiting process. What if, instead of talking about recruitment speed, the team talks abut the latest indicators showing how the top performers feel about their jobs and the company? That focus would lead to an entirely different set of conversations and actions.

Metrics enable you and your team to discuss your part of the business with some accuracy and specificity. Your conversations will be richer and make a greater difference when enhanced by the knowledge of good metrics. When you create measurement practices, you're putting the metrics into your daily and weekly regimens— inviting the data into the department as a respected partner. Here are a few examples of ways to create measurement practices:

- involve the entire team in selecting and measuring indicators
- measure results on a regular basis—the same every month—so that it becomes a habit
- talk about metrics at team meetings—don't just review them; engage in meaty conversation about what the metrics are telling you and your team members
- post metrics—on common walls, on your office walls, on the intranet
- acknowledge and celebrate successes.

If you and your team are crystal-clear about the results you need to achieve (as you defined them in Step 2), have crisp metrics that tell you how you're doing. If you regularly discuss these metrics, your results will improve. We get what we pay attention to.

Managing on the Basis of Your Metrics

To manage on the basis of metrics means letting the data influence decisions, changes, and practices. If the data are telling you that you're not producing adequate results, you need to change what you're doing. This might mean letting go of work that others think is making a difference.

Here's a great example. I heard the esteemed educator and public advocate Geoffrey Canada speak at a leadership conference, and he offered this amazing story of the power of managing based on metrics. Canada has spent his career trying to help inner-city youth better their lives through education. As the program director for the Truancy Prevention Program in New York City, he was revered as a great leader and an amazingly positive influence on the local kids. He and his team worked very hard and were well regarded. Then Canada started noticing that their results were inadequate and that their hard work didn't seem to be making a difference. In New York City, 50 percent of African American males were unemployed and 350,000 kids had not graduated from high school. These statistics were troubling and signaled that there was a big systemic problem that was not being addressed.

Canada shifted his definition of success. He looked at the work he and his organization were doing, and he determined they were not making an acceptable impact on the number of kids who graduated from high school and went on to attend college. They had many popular programs in the community, but Canada saw that his work wasn't producing the results he sought. When he shared his new metrics and the disappointing results, most people defended Canada and his organization and tried to convince him that he was doing a great job. But he knew the facts didn't support that approbation. He decided to make drastic changes, which resulted in the Harlem Children's Zone—a comprehensive program that helps children and parents from the time a child is born until he or she goes to college. This initiative was new and bold, and people said it couldn't be done. But Canada persevered and made it happen. And the results have been amazing. In the 2003/04 school year, 86 percent of the high school seniors within the Harlem Children's Zone were accepted to a college. (By contrast, only 70 percent of New York City seniors, in

POINTER

Metrics exist to help you make better business decisions. Sometimes this may mean making large adjustments to projects, processes, and practices. If something isn't working, you need to make a change or fix it.

general, planned to go to college.) When he started the Children's Zone, as many as 80 percent of Harlem school kids had fallen behind in school. Canada's success has been profiled by many news outlets, including CBS' "60 Minutes" and in the *New York Times*. Other children's zones are developing, based on his model. The long-term impact of his work to New York City, the country, and the world will be tough to measure, but certainly immense. And the key breakthrough for Canada was managing based on metrics.

Imagine the impact you and your team can make if you focus on the right measures and align your practices for success! As managers, we might need to see that some of our well-intended efforts are not making a difference—even if other people think they are and tell you that you and your team are doing a great job. Managing based on metrics means having the courage and conviction to adjust the work to produce the desired results. This is gut-check time.

Tune Up and Realign Strategy for Step 3

◆ To ensure you're tuned up, go through Worksheet 3.1 with your team and then share the results with your manager to make sure that the two of you are thinking along the same lines.

◆ Think about the two examples I discuss in this step, and make sure that there aren't any elements (like total costs) that you're leaving out of your metrics.

NOTES

Build a Great Team

OVERVIEW

Creating connections

Enlivening minds

Cultivating productive irreverence

Reinforcing collaboration

I think that many traditional in-dicators of a good team ought to be retired. I've had managers tell me they loved their teams be-cause everyone was cooperative and got along well—their teams gave them no problems. Perfor-mance evaluation forms define a good team player as one who pitches in to help and doesn't create conflict. When people buck the system, we tell them they're not playing nice. I say this is all bunk!

I want a team of people who will not hesitate to challenge each other or me. I want productive conflict because that's how we grow and learn. I want the team to be a pain in the neck sometimes—business is a contact sport. I'm not looking for amiable and compli-ant team members—I want spunk, passion, sharpness, and occa-sional anger. That's what a great and energized team looks like to me, and I think you could benefit from that kind of team, too. Be-fore you send me a bunch of angry emails, let me say that I like niceness, too. I would like people to enjoy working together and to help each other out, but that's not the only thing I'm looking for in my team.

As managers, we create the work environment and we determine whether we get the team members described in the first or the second paragraph above—the nice team or the energized and nice team. What we do each day, how we respond to diversity, and what staffing choices we make communicate the type of team behaviors we're seeking. If we embrace and reinforce compliance, we'll get lots of it. If we show sincere gratitude when people are candid about concerns, we'll get more candor from everyone on the team. When we promote the productive troublemaker, we send a big message to everyone on the team that it's OK to express real feelings and beliefs.

Creating Connections

Business is a contact sport and management is a social act. Until the robots take over, we need to get things done through people. And what that really means is that our relationships are the conduits for results. Think of a complicated telephone switch box with wires running to each home and then to the telephone company. There are wires of different colors, some with stripes; some are hot, some ground the current. Wires everywhere making each conversation happen. If a wire gets kinked, cut, or corroded, the conversations stop. Your team is like that box, and making sure you have each relationship wired and maintained is critical to ensuring the right conversations are able to occur.

Team members who know each other work better together. They care about each other's successes and are more likely to put up a big stink if things aren't going well. That's what we want—people looking out for each other and bringing potential problems to the fore. Tolerance, trust, respect, collaboration, and even anger, challenge, and confrontation come from knowing. We need to make sure our team members get to know each other, even if they're located in different countries or speak different languages. With the communication options we have available today, there's no reason a team of peers can't develop deep and productive work relationships.

To create the connection is basic—people need to spend time getting to know one another. I'm not advocating a bunch of sit-in-a-corner-chanting team-building sessions or outdoor ropes classes or off-site golf outings. Those get-togethers are OK, but not necessary. I do like facilitated behavioral-style team sessions—like using the MBTI (Myers-Briggs Type Indicator)—but otherwise recommend that you get to know each other by talking about the business. The business is what binds you to one another. If people have robust and open conversations about the business during their team meetings and morning huddles, you'll find that they'll also have more informal conversations during other times. IF you pepper in a few informal team conversations and bring in Krispy Kremes and vanilla lattes, you'll find that people begin to connect—the sugar and caffeine help and are fun.

STEP 4

Be careful about the signals you send your team members because sometimes our efforts can cause an unintended reaction. Coddling people who have clashes of personality is a well-intended act that ends up hurting relationships. Variety adds spice and I hope that you have a team filled with people so different they might not want to go bowling together. That said, I've seen very dissimilar people enjoy a game of bowling. Business is business, and we don't have the luxury of working only with those people toward whom we naturally gravitate. In fact, that would be bad for business.

As a manager, you should model productive work relationships with all types of people and not tolerate immaturity from others. That's right, immaturity. We all have a job to do and we might need to partner with someone distasteful to us—get over it and do great work!

> **POINTER**
>
> Management is a social act. Managers ought to be master conversationalists and focus on helping their teams build deep and intimate relationships.

People rise to our expectations, so expect that all team members will develop and maintain deep work relationships. Structure your day and week to reinforce and model this goal. Here are a few examples of how to create team connections:

◆ Begin holding morning huddles for 5–10 minutes so that everyone can check in with each other. Over time, huddling will strengthen mutual trust and understanding.

◆ If you have a company lunchroom, make it a point to eat there most days, sitting with peers and team members. Create a positive group conversation.

◆ Talk about the importance of building deep work relationships, and begin every team meeting with business-related questions that prompt each person to share something about his or her experience, opinions, or ideas.

◆ Hold more group brainstorming sessions.

◆ Assign some tasks to pairs and trios. Over time, make sure that everyone pairs up with everyone else.

◆ Ask the training department to facilitate a session about behavioral styles. There are many easy and inexpensive assessments you can use for this purpose, like the MBTI, the DISC Profile, the Social Style Model, and Activity Vector Analysis.

◆ Increase the likelihood that team members will converse through their assignments, physical location, meetings, and schedules.

◆ A team that feels connected by a common goal or mission will relate more deeply. Make sure that your team members know why they're here and why they're here together.

Creating relationships takes time so don't be cheap when it comes to ensuring your team spends time together. Sure, each individual has a specific job to do, but each person's success depends on how well individual efforts come together. Great managers are relationship builders.

Enlivening Your Team Members' Minds

What's the purpose for a team? Why is a team structure of any advantage? Why don't we just have individual contributors who do their own things? The only reason to have a team and to develop a team is to benefit from the members' abilities to think and work together, strengthen interest and commitment, and thereby make the organization stronger and more successful. That's it; that's why we have teams.

As team managers, we need to ensure that team members do great work together. Team work is a social act, just like management is a social act. The work of teams occurs in conversation—all that teams can do is think, collaborate, decide, and coordinate or plan. And it all starts with good thinking by enlivened minds.

I can't count the times that I've seen intelligent and hard-working people performing far below their potential. I'd bet you've seen this, too. Sometimes it's a problem of burnout or maybe the person is in the wrong job. Most of the time, however, it's a management problem. The degree to which our team members' minds are engaged in their work is a direct reflection of our management effectiveness. In other words, it's our fault either way. Individuals might get into a funk every now and then—that's normal. But if you have people on your team who are just going through the motions, you have a systemic management challenge.

I hate to keep throwing this back on you, but enlivening minds begins with role modeling. Is your mind alive and engaged? If not, you need to fix that right now because no one wants to get excited about working for an uninspired manager. Tool 4.1 suggests several ways you can enliven minds at work.

Cultivating Productive Irreverence

When we're irreverent, we show a lack of respect for people or things. *Productive* irreverence, however, is showing a lack of respect for things, processes, practices, and tasks that *ought to change* so the team can make progress. I'm not advocating that team members demonstrate a lack of respect for one another, but I am encouraging a lack of respect for projects that no longer make sense. Productive irreverence is needed to ensure that you and your team members

TOOL 4.1

Ways to Enliven Minds at Work

Focus Area	Enlivening Technique
Connection to the company	Be as transparent with company information as you possibly can. Keep your team informed. Share their feedback with peers and your manager so they feel their voices have been heard.
Energy	Have quick and energetic huddles instead of meetings. Be energetic yourself. Encourage people to get up and move around throughout the day. Hire high-energy people. Help team members manage stress, and make sure no one is working too many hours on a consistent basis.
Participation in team conversations	Ask provocative and evocative questions. Elicit everyone's input and show your gratitude for ideas, even contrary ones. Ask people to comment on topics that you know interest them. Send out questions before meetings so people can prepare their thoughts.
Collaboration	Ask for team or subteam recommendations. Put people into pairs and small groups to work on projects. Acknowledge and reinforce group accomplishment.

are questioning practices and tasks that ought to be questioned. Someone who is productively irreverent is an occasional trouble-maker and a person you want on your team—more than one would be even better.

Another aspect of being productively irreverent is knowing when and how to communicate concerns and knowing when to keep concerns to yourself. I love occasional troublemakers, I really do. That said, too much is too much! Productive irreverence is selective. I've coached several less-than-selective folks about how to pick their battles for maximum influence and impact.

As the manager, how do you cultivate productive irreverence? Here are two powerful strategies. I bet you can guess the first one—

model productive irreverence yourself. Make sure that you challenge the status quo when challenge is warranted and show impatience with continuing to do the wrong things. Managers have told me that their work environment doesn't tolerate productive irreverence. I wonder why that is? Of the people who say this, perhaps 5 percent are stuck—they work for the top-paying employer, need the work to feed their kids, or work in an environment where compliance matters more than contribution. Honestly, this book is not written for people who work in that type of environment. And I believe that most managers—the other 95 percent or so—would improve their reputation, not harm it, by being productively irreverent.

Here's a bonus: Being productively irreverent is so much fun! It's fun because breakthroughs can occur when we help our managers, peers, or team members see something in a new way. Breakthroughs are cool. Think about your current list of projects. I bet one or more of those projects ought to be changed or killed. What a relief it would be for the team and business if you crossed irrelevant projects off their lists of worries. And that relates to enlivening the mind as well because working on a stupid project feels stupid—and draining—and it's no fun.

Here's how you become productively irreverent. Look back at Steps 1, 2, and 3. Ask yourself if there are tasks, projects, or processes that are taking up people's time and energy but not directly supporting the results you're being asked to produce. Evaluate everything, even small things like reports, meetings, approvals required, or documentation. In some productive way each day, question one action or task with the appropriate people. Here's an example of how you might tee up that conversation:

> We all have way too much on our to-do lists, and I want to do my part in helping us reduce the activities that might no longer make sense relative to our other priorities. I did a quick map of the process we use to get product specifications to the marketing department. Everyone's frustrated with how long this takes, and it's nobody's fault. The process is just very long, and I think

there might be a couple places where we can cut steps and make everyone happier.

I call someone who is productively irreverent a *prodIR* (sounds like "prodder"). Effective prodIRs share their intent first—always something along the lines of making everyone's work life easier and more productive. ProdIRs are a bit like beauty pageant contestants: they always want to create world peace. Productive irreverence is all about making the work planet a lot better. The power of this effort is that when we improve our workplace, everyone raises his or her game.

That's how you become a prodIR—start small and start having well-intended, open, and positive conversations that ask, Why? But don't get upset if people defend the status quo and decide they want to keep things as they are. Do your best job of explaining the potential opportunities for improvement and keep plugging away (remember, remember, you still need to be selective to some extent).

Never go negative—that's not productive; it's just plain irreverent. I had a manager pal who'd occasionally blow a gasket if he didn't get his way when he brought up things he thought needed to change. Such immaturity hurt his ability to influence peers and managers and got in the way of his career. Eventually, he overcame this derailing factor—and that was great because had he not changed, he would have become more of a troublemaker than the business could tolerate.

The second strategy for cultivating productive irreverence is to ask for it. Seek all kinds of input and show you're thankful for challenging questions, concerns, and diverse ideas. Call it productive irreverence and ask for it by name when you meet with your team. This will help some members get over the fear of sharing their concerns. Ask for ideas that might seem crazy or impossible. Make it a routine to ask your team members for the tasks on their list that they think aren't worth the effort. Show gratitude, no matter which tasks they identify. Ask clarifying questions to better understand why the task is of low value. Hire people you know will challenge you. Promote employees who take the initiative to try to improve processes and practices, even when doing so might involve bringing up a sensitive topic (like your pet project). If an employee questions your pet project—great! Really, it's great because if it's your pet project, it's important to you and therefore important to do well.

Reinforcing Collaboration

Most managers will say they want collaboration, but few act consistent with those words. When we set goals, are they individual or team goals? When you fill out a performance evaluation, are you rating individual or team performance? What are the criteria for promotions, pay raises, and bonuses—individual accomplishments or team accomplishments? I'm not suggesting that acknowledging and reinforcing individual excellence isn't a good thing—you should reinforce it. But it's important to notice the balance of what you're reinforcing so you can determine to what degree your actions and words match your intentions.

People collaborate more when they're given the time, when it's easy to communicate with peers and team members, when they've had the opportunity or practice at working with others, and when they gain a feeling of satisfaction and accomplishment from working together. How many of those conditions exist in your work environment? You can help create the place for all those conditions.

I was talking to a team manager for a software company. He'd done a research project that looked at the effectiveness of project teams. His research showed that the teams who collaborated outperformed the teams who didn't—five to one. Collaborating teams were five times more productive and successful than their noncollaborating peers. I'm not sure you would see that same five-to-one difference in performance, but I am sure that you would see a significant increase in productivity and results if you increased collaboration. He's a big advocate for seating teams together when possible—like in a square of cubicles facing inward with a team meeting table in the middle. This may not be possible or practical in your

POINTER

Your team will perform better when they collaborate. Make sure your actions and words encourage effective collaboration.

workplace, but it's good to look at how easy or difficult it is for teams to communicate. Personally, I like letting the team get involved with how their workplace should be arranged.

When I was at Black & Decker (B&D), I was part of an international crossfunctional product development initiative. At B&D, the product development teams were global, which meant that many team members never saw each other. That made it difficult to encourage collaboration and effective communication. B&D wanted to improve and shorten the product development life cycle, so it got all the global teams together for a four-day training program. One of the best outcomes of that training initiative was that teams met and were able to build relationships and agree on the best ways to communicate and collaborate. B&D was very successful in improving its development process, and its next large new line of power tools—the DeWalt line—was a huge success for the company. Collaboration and communication were key to that success, and they will be key to yours. Tool 4.2 offers several ways you can reinforce collaboration.

One other idea is to hand out provocative articles or blog posts to get people talking. Once they get into conversation, team members will transition more naturally into collaborating on specific business issues or opportunities.

Tune Up and Realign Strategy for Step 4

◆ Do a quick assessment of the team elements presented in this step: How strong are the relationships among team members (and with you)? Are your people's minds actively engaged? Do you have an environment of productive irreverence? Are you productively irreverent? Do team members regularly collaborate?

TOOL 4.2

Ways to Produce and Reinforce Collaboration

Factor	Ideas for Producing and Reinforcing Collaboration
Physical location	House teams together or in a way that encourages informal conversation. Make sure that informal meeting spaces are available. If the team is located in more than one place, get members together on a regular basis and encourage them to use technology to have both informal and planned conversations. Give them unrestricted access to phone, email, Internet phone, teleconferencing services, and web seminar software.
Communication processes	Make it a habit to use a portion of your team meetings for collaboration. When people come to your office with questions or ideas, encourage them to gather a few peers to talk through the issue (eventually, they'll do this before coming to you—a beautiful thing).
Tasks and assignments	Assign projects and tasks to teams, subteams, and pairs of peers. Get your team in the habit of working together.
Goals and measurements	Make sure that at least half of your employees' goals are team, subteam, or pair goals. Use team measures along with individual measures for any evaluations, pay raise considerations, promotions, and bonuses. (I don't recommend linking evaluations to pay raises.)
Workplace culture	Reinforce and show appreciation for collaborative work. Model collaboration by asking team members and peers to work with you on your tasks and projects. Encourage diverse opinions and points of view. Show support when team members get together for informal conversations or meetings.

STEP 4

◆ Based on your assessment, go back to any section in the step that seems to need improvement, and try a few of the techniques I recommend. All of the techniques produce a common outcome—they facilitate people spending quality time together and creating better business conversations.

◆ Embrace your role as a master conversationalist and make every meeting and conversation a great one.

Choose Employees Wisely

There are few things in this world that I know for sure, and this is one: Our ability to hire the right people for our job openings will influence our success more than most other management actions. Hiring right is critical. When we have the right team of people, we have the time and flexibility to do our best management work. So much of what takes up many managers' days is compensating for not hiring right. It's important to be very picky when hiring, and we don't want to settle on someone who's not the right fit for the position. Let me repeat the important words again—*right fit for the position* (and organization). Your objective is not to find the highest IQ or greatest number of years of experience; it's to find the right person for a particular job at a particular time.

One of the most effective ways to reduce the need for counseling or termination conversations is to hire the right people in the first place. Most terminations are the result of poor fit with the position. The desire to fill open positions may tempt busy managers to accept marginal candidates, but that's never the best solution or the right thing to do. Never! Keep your job-fit standards and

POINTER

Finding someone who's the right fit for your open position is more important than finding the person who has the most experience or seems the brightest.

expectations high. The right person can infuse the team with positive energy and valuable skills.

Defining Job-Fit Criteria

How do I write this politely and with some level of political correctness? Oh, forget about it; I'll just type what I'm thinking—most job descriptions suck. They suck for a few reasons. First, most job descriptions don't describe the most important aspects of the job. If you were to write a paragraph detailing the most important work you do (important because of its impact on the business), and if you then compared what you wrote with the description of your job on file in the HR department, would they be the same? Not likely—but they ought to be.

Here's another reason I hate most job descriptions: They don't help you find the rock star. Think about the most amazing employee at your company. Do you believe that person's background and experiences match his or her job description? Most don't and, in fact, some applicants wouldn't even get an interview if the job description were used as the only screening criterion. In other words, job descriptions often do a disservice to the selection process.

Finally, job descriptions generally don't address job fit, or the type of person you're seeking for the role. Bottom line? Writing a job description is not the same as defining criteria for job fit. Answer these questions to determine job-fit characteristics:

◆ What type of person will best be able to have amazing success in this role, given the tasks, the team dynamics, the work environment, and the areas of organization dysfunction?

◆ With thought to people who've done this work in the past, what beliefs and behaviors were most successful, which were least successful, and why?

STEP 5

- Over the next year, what changes or improvements do I hope to see the person in this role own or lead? What type of person will be most successful at making those changes happen?
- Given the relative strengths and weaknesses of the other team members, what type of person would best help the team rise to the next level of performance? What skills and experiences does the team need?
- What type of person will best challenge me and help push our department forward?
- Why is the candidate interested in the job, and what are her or his career goals? Does this position make sense as the next position in her or his desired progression? If not, why is the candidate interested; and, if hired, will he or she stay?

I do a lot of contract recruiting, particularly for management positions. The reason my clients call me again and again is that they find it difficult to determine fit—or determine when someone is *not* a fit. That's their greater challenge—they often think the person is a great candidate because of experience and background. Most of the time, however, the person is not a fit. Think about this statement because it's the way it ought to be: Most people are not a fit for your open jobs. Think about five businesses in your home city. Most of them would *not* be a great fit for you—even within similar industries. For example, here in Seattle we have two large coffee companies—Starbucks and Tully's. I've often thought I'd like to work with Tully's, but not Starbucks. Why? I like a scrappy entrepreneurial environment, and Tully's seems to fit that more than Starbucks. I think Starbucks has gotten so big so fast that it might be harder to have an impact (like steering the Titanic). We all have different work environments that will be a great fit. When we interview candidates, we need to have the environment and fit in mind so we can better select the best person. If you don't take the time to define the criteria for job fit, you'll have no way to know how well each candidate matches up with what you're seeking.

Interviewing Deeply and Well

Here's a quiz question for you: Is a job interview a test or a conversation?

Do you shine a bright light in the eyes of hopeful candidates or subject them to firing squads of five-on-one group interviews? Do you hope that you'll ask the question that trips candidates up so you can eliminate them? An interview ought to be a conversation—a two-way discussion that lets you get to know the candidate, and vice versa.

I'm not a fan of group interviews because they don't make for a good conversation. Relationships are not being built, and you're subjecting the candidate to stress that might inhibit his or her ability to open up and share experiences. I once was interviewed by a group of 12 people. The group included the CEO and several members of his senior leadership team. As a facilitator, I was able to handle the conversation. I was determined to get the job—for one reason, because I wanted to get them to stop doing these group interviews! Did I really get to know any of them? No. Did they really get to know me? No. All they learned was that I could facilitate a conversation with 12 people.

Here are a few other recommendations for how to interview deeply and well, and find the candidate who's the best fit for your open positions:

◆ First and foremost, **don't let HR own the process of filling your position.** Too many managers abdicate ownership of hiring, and it's a big mistake. Who needs to train this person? Who needs to manage this person? Who'll be responsible for ensuring this person is productive? On whose team will this person reside? You and yours. Personally, I would not even let HR narrow the candidates to a list you ought to interview. There might be one of those unconventional rock stars in the pile of résumés, and HR departments are more likely to screen based on job descriptions. Take the time to be very involved from the get-go. Nothing against HR; I've been an HR person myself. But HR doesn't know your needs and team like you do, and HR won't be managing the hire. It's in your best interest to get and stay involved. I know that some government agencies don't let managers own the initial screening—if you work for the government, be as involved as your system allows, and advocate for improving the system in an appropriate manner.

◆ **Use behavioral interviewing.** I like using behavior-based questions because they tell you how people approach their work and how they respond to various situations. Example 5.1 lists several behavioral interviewing questions I've used when talking to candidates for management positions.

◆ **Don't overmanage how your interviewers use behavioral interview questions.** I'm not a fan of using behavioral questions in such a regimented way that they hinder conversation and relationship. Do you hand interviewers a list of seven questions and tell them to ask only those and nothing else? I don't recommend that approach—it's mechanical, and hiring a rock star needs to be a bit magical, too. (I can imagine all the employment attorneys wrinkling their noses at me while reading that.) I think it's fine to ask each candidate some of the same questions, but then also take time for conversation that's specific to experiences and interests. If you're not skilled in interviewing techniques, seek training or coaching because competence at interviewing is necessary to make the right people decisions.

◆ When talking to each candidate, **get to know her or his motivation for submitting an application.** What does he or she want to get from the position? What work does she or he most enjoy? If you're hiring a manager, determine whether the candidate has a genuine interest in and capacity for management—mere managing experience is not enough. You and I know there are many lousy managers out there!

◆ **Ask several people to interview each candidate—one-on-one.** Make sure the interviewers know your criteria for fit. Have a group debriefing meeting to get feedback. If

EXAMPLE 5.1

Sample Behavioral Questions for a Management Position Interview

1. Each member of a leadership team brings unique strengths and weaknesses. For the last/current leadership team you belonged to,
   a. describe the team—its size, members.
   b. describe the unique skills and talents that you brought to the team *beyond* your functional knowledge.
   c. describe the ways in which you relied on other team members for coaching and advice.

2. What do you think are the ideal composition and function of a leadership team? How often should it meet? What should the focus of its meetings be? How else should members work together? What authority/ownership should members assert with each other?

3. Describe a time when you asserted yourself at a regular leadership team meeting. What was the situation? What did you say? What were the results?

4. Describe the two contributions you made in the last year that you are most proud of? How have these contributions helped the company?

5. Beyond your functional projects and tasks, in what ways have you helped the company improve its ability to manage, execute, and react to change?

6. Tell me about a peer with whom you have had the most difficulty working? What made it difficult? What did you do about it? What were the results?

7. If we were to ask your current/last peers and manager to describe the greatest strengths you brought to the company, what do you think they would say? Why?

8. Over the next two years, how would you like to grow as a leader? How will you approach getting this development?

9. Over the last year, what was the largest problem you had to solve? How did you approach it? What did you do? What were the results?

10. Describe your leadership and management style. How do you ensure everyone on your team is working on the right stuff? How do you communicate? What's your belief about what makes people perform their best?

11. As a member of the leadership team, the [open position title] needs to communicate fully but appropriately with his or her teams, peers, and managers. How would you approach that responsibility? What, if anything, should be off-limits? What do team members need to know, and what do peers and managers need to know?

someone has a bad or really good feeling about a candidate, take that seriously and look into it further. Our instincts are often right.

♦ **Make sure you give candidates lots of time to ask questions.** It's important that they have an opportunity to get to know you and learn what they need to determine their level of interest. I also think you can tell a lot about how a candidate thinks by the questions he or she asks. If there are no questions, that's a concern to me. If all the questions are about pay and benefits, that's a red flag, too. I want to hire someone who's interested in the business—interested enough to have done some research and come to the interview with several business-related queries.

One last thought before I move on to another topic. The interview process is about establishing a relationship. That relationship begins before the first interview occurs. I know that many of you may not have a lot of say about how applications are collected and screened, but I want you to consider the message your company sends if the only way candidates can apply for a job is online, and there's no email address or phone number that connects to a human who's available to answer questions. If that's the way your HR department recruits, do whatever you can to get them to change their tactics. Such a cold and inaccessible system will hurt your hiring efforts because the rock stars will have no patience for the system, and many of the folks who take the time to fight through the system won't be the best applicants. That's my two cents worth.

Taking Reference Checks Seriously

Conduct thorough reference checks! Many managers think checking references is a waste of time, but that's not true if it's done well. Even discussions with references provided by the candidate (presumably, her or his allies) can be illuminating. Here's the thing: You get a list of references from a candidate. We should assume that these people are professional friends. In other words, you're going to get a positive reference. So why bother? Even friends don't lie very well, and what they'll tell you is the most prominent strengths and relative weaknesses.

References will often help break a tie between two strong candidates or confirm a nagging feeling about the person's background. I once did reference checks for a director-level role. We were down to two candidates and both were very strong. For this position, we needed a change agent to make big improvements in the way the department was structured and run. The reference checks made our decision clear. As I talked to each candidate's work pals, important differences emerged that we also suspected during the interview phase. One man had more experience and was a steady manager, but he wasn't a change agent. The second man was less experienced, but change and results were his strong suits. The candidates' friends told me this. We hired the change agent and never looked back—it was the best hire of the year. Tool 5.1 offers several reference questions I've used successfully in the past.

TOOL 5.1

Reference Check Questions and Why You Should Ask Them

Question	Why Ask This Question
How did you know this person? On what types of projects did you work together?	To better understand their professional relationship and get a feel for how well the reference remembers the candidate.
Tell me about [candidate name]'s job. What did he or she do while at [company name]?	To get a feel for how well the candidate's description of the job matches what the reference remembers.
Everyone has special talents—things they do better than others. What did [candidate name] do better than most people at the company?	This will give you a feel for the candidate's greatest strengths. That's important because those strengths will be the key attributes that you'll be buying if you hire the person. Are these the strengths you most need right now?

Tool 5.1, continued

Question	Why Ask This Question
We all get stressed every now and then. What tended to stress out [candidate name]?	This is a way of asking about weaknesses and of learning what type of environment will set the candidate off. It's a critical question to determine fit.
We obviously think highly of [candidate name]. If we extend an offer and if the offer is accepted, what would your advice be to [candidate name]'s new manager for how to get the best performance from [candidate name]?	I love this question. Believe it or not, most references, even the close buddies, are totally honest here. This is where you learn what kind of management a candidate will require and whether the candidate leans toward independence or dependence, high or low maintenance. These are important fit issues.
If you had another position open, would you hire [candidate name] again? Why/why not?	The reference likely will say "yes," but notice whether and for how long he or she hesitates. If the "yes" is immediate, that's great. If it takes a while or if the "yes" is qualified with a statement like, "Well, my company doesn't do that kind of work anymore," that's not so good.
For management candidates: Aside from functional expertise, in what ways did [candidate name] add to the effectiveness of the leadership team?	This will tell you the candidate's contribution to the management team. If the reference offers nothing beyond the candidate's functional expertise (the reference will struggle to answer the question), take a pass on the applicant. You need someone who'll strengthen the team in many ways.
For management candidates: How did [candidate name] maximize team performance. How did she or he ensure the team was doing its best work?	The reference may struggle with this one, but it will likely give you some insight into the candidate's management style. If the reference says he or she doesn't know, that's likely not true and may be a red flag.

STEP 5

Getting Excited about Your Choice

When you select a candidate, rejoice and celebrate! You have a new team member who will bring new energy and talent to the work environment. It's important that your new hire and your team can feel

POINTER

Reference checks can be very helpful in determining a candidate's relative strengths and weaknesses.

your energy for this person. You want your new hire to feel special, welcome, and needed—the candidate you select *is* special. With every new hire, you communicate again—to all team members—the behaviors and talents that you seek and value. This is a time when you can reinforce your expectations and reenergize the team. Get the new member of your team off to a great start with lots of support and enthusiasm. And start building relationships early by asking various team members to participate in orienting the new guy or gal.

If no candidate is a great fit, keep looking. Don't settle for a person who's merely available and convenient. In the end, doing so won't benefit the organization or the person hired. Managers who are picky about the people they bring onto their team will enjoy better results than their less selective peers. Each hiring decision communicates what you and the organization are looking for and what behaviors and skills are most desirable.

Tune Up and Realign Strategy for Step 5

- ◆ Are you taking enough time with candidates?
- ◆ Are you building relationships during the interview process?
- ◆ Evaluate the effectiveness of your last couple of hires. Is hindsight 20/20, and would you have made the same decision if you'd known then what you know now about the candidate?
- ◆ If you have some work to do to improve your hiring, work with the HR department to make the next recruiting process deeper and more detailed.
- ◆ Take some time to define the job-fit criteria for an open position.

◆ Spend more time and involve more people in the interviewing process, particularly if the open position has turned over more than once in the last three years.

◆ Check out the behavioral questions and sample reference check questions I've offered.

NOTES

N O T E S

_____

_____

_____

_____

_____

_____

_____

_____

_____

_____

_____

_____

_____

_____

_____

_____

_____

_____

_____

_____

_____

_____

_____

Define and Model Excellence

Excellence. It's a lofty word that we throw around a lot in training courses and books like this. It's too bad that we don't talk more about excellence. Excellent performance, after all, is very, very good! A common reason why we don't see more excellent performance is that we don't talk about what excellence really looks like and how we would know it if we saw it in action.

Talking about excellence is powerful. Conversations create reality. Spend time talking about excellence, and you'll likely get more excellent performance from your team members. It really works that way—amazing! People make individual choices about what to do and how to do it based on their understanding of expectations and their individual motivations. Managers want to make sure that the filter individuals are using is a good one.

There's one snag or trouble spot: To talk more about excellence, we need to *define* excellence and describe it in ways that bring it to life. Saying "excellence is doing a great job" is a cop-out; it's not helpful. Defining *excellence* is a wonderful exercise that all managers should do every few months.

Defining Excellence

In Steps 1 and 2, you discovered what excellence looks like for your position, and you defined the contribution your manager expects you and your group to make to the organization. Now it's time to create that same view and focus for your team's performance. Imagine that your team is thriving and performing at the top of its game. Now look around and write down what you see. How are people communicating? How do people spend their time? What happens when problems arise? In what ways are team members showing creativity? Want kind of innovation do you see happening? Describe what it looks like when projects exceed expectations. What does learning and relationship building look like?

Put together a one-page description of excellence for your department and then add a paragraph or two for each unique position. It's fine to involve your team members in creating a vision of excellence, but your team members need to know how *you* define it.

To give you an idea of the behavioral description that I recommend you create, here's an example. It's a real definition of excellence that I created with a client company for its management team (and I've removed the company name and proprietary information below):

Managerial excellence at ABCo:

◆ You and your team are focused on what's most important, and you produce excellent results. People work at a brisk pace, but they do not feel burned out. Employees are clear about priorities and how their work ties to departmental and corporate goals.

◆ Your work environment encourages team members to do their best work and execute well. They feel challenged and important. Communication is open, candid, and focused on the business. Although they know they are accountable for results, employees are driven by their intrinsic motivation to excel and accomplish.

◈ You know time is a precious resource and you ensure that your team and you use it wisely. Meetings are called only when necessary, and they are well run. Conversations are lively, provocative, evocative, and focused. People are eager to participate in business dialogue and to contribute their ideas and concerns. You and your team have become master conversationalists. Even so, you do not bog people down with unnecessary meetings, emails, conference calls, or written material.

◈ You know that saying "no" is just as important as saying "yes." You demonstrate focus and courage to make sure that your team does not get buried with projects or tasks that are nice to do but would not make it to the list of what's most important. You productively partner with your manager and peers to choose collectively the work that will best support the company's goals and reject projects that do not. Your focus helps you and your team produce results and serve your internal and external customers.

◈ You have tuned your department to best serve the needs of your internal and external customers. You aggressively eliminate barriers to providing outstanding service, and you reengineer processes and practices that support your operations. You acknowledge the importance of serving internal customers such that external customers are better served and satisfied. You work proactively with peers to ensure that interdepartmental processes and practices are effective.

◈ The only constant is change. You and your team are able to respond nimbly to changing needs and conditions. You respond to emerging needs and do not hesitate to readjust tasks and work flow when needed. You help your team adjust and come to terms with change.

◆ You know you are the face of ABCo and play an important role in helping the company grow and mature. You model excellence and are a pleasure to work with. You are regarded as trustworthy and reliable. Employees want to be a member of your team, and they know you will support their needs and goals. You take administrative responsibilities seriously and complete forms and reports on time. As an agent for the company, you make good judgments on its behalf and protect it from unacceptable risk.

This is what managerial excellence looks like, and we know that each of our managers is capable of achieving this level of contribution. Some of you might need to question a few habits or learn new skills. The journey will be well worth it. Imagine what work will feel like when you reach managerial excellence. The impact you will have on the organization will be inspiring and significant in terms of tangible results. You will feel like you make a difference every day. Strong teams will stay together and do great work. ABCo will be a better, stronger, and more sought-after company—by prospective employees and customers.

POINTER

Your team needs to know how *you* define excellent performance.

What do you think? As a manager, does reading this description give you any ideas for how you can make a positive contribution every day? Your definition of excellence ought to be inspiring and challenging—you're going for excellence, after all; not mediocrity. Once you've defined excellence, shout it out from the top of the building! Use worksheet 6.1 to help create your vision of excellence for your function and your team.

WORKSHEET 6.1

Defining Excellence

Instructions: Describe performance excellence for each performance factor.

Performance Factor	How You Define Excellence for This Factor
Communication	
Collaboration	
Professionalism	
Creativity and innovation	
Project performance	
Meetings	
Problem identifying and solving	
Change and agility	
Results and performance	
Team and organization	

Communicating the Definition of Excellence

Let's start this section with tips for how *not* to communicate your definition of excellence. Don't share excellence like it's the minimum expectation and those who aren't there either aren't pulling their load or are missing a few important brain cells. Try not to describe excellent performance the way a drill sergeant would bark mess hall duties. Don't create a spreadsheet with boxes, checkmarks, Xs, and spaces to fill. Don't put excellence into SMART (specific, measurable, attainable, relevant, timeframe) goal terms.

Excellence is a vision. It's a wonderful picture of what things are like when everything clicks and hums. Excellence is a story—not an assignment.

Here's how I share my vision of excellence with my team. First I gather them all together in a meeting room and schedule the meeting for one hour. I bring muffins if the meeting is in the morning and cookies in the afternoon. I let my team know that it's always good to understand where each member is coming from regarding beliefs about how we can best do our work; and that I believe it's helpful for each team member to know how I define excellence. I share my vision of excellence in detail. Then I ask for reactions and questions, inviting people to share their thoughts about excellence. I show my gratitude for their input. I let them know that, personally and as the manager of the team, I want to shoot for excellence and I hope they do, too. I let the team know it can depend on me to give honest and frequent feedback, and that I will appreciate the energy and passion team members pour into the work.

You should communicate your definition of excellence in a way that's consistent with your style, but (1) make sure you're specific in describing your vision; (2) describe excellence in a way that inspires your team; and (3) invite input, reactions, and open conversation. Once you've defined excellence, make sure that you read and refer to your vision every week. You need to stay connected to your vision and find ways to keep your team connected as well.

At the start of meetings, take five minutes to read and refresh the vision of excellence. When people bring up ideas, questions, and concerns, ask for alternatives that would best support excellence.

POINTER

Passionately communicate your definition of excellence, using specifics that enable people to form a mental picture of excellence in action.

Acting Consistently with Your Definition of Excellence

Your ability to communicate a vision of excellence and to improve performance can be hampered by actions that contradict your vision. Do you say that you want to create an environment where productive and energetic conversations occur during meetings—but then put your team through the usual and dreaded go-around-the-table staff meetings? Do you say excellence means that everyone contributes ideas and has the opportunity to lead—but then bog your people down in routine tasks and offer no forum for sharing ideas?

One of the most difficult aspects of management is the demand that we behave consistently with our goals, visions, and the behaviors we want to see in others. We don't get to be confusing or immature; demonstrating poor judgment isn't one of our options. Being consistent is difficult and falling back into comfortable habits that might not serve us well is easier. We need to think about what we're doing each day and ensure that it's in alignment with how we want to influence performance.

POINTER

Make sure your actions don't inadvertently contradict your definition of excellence.

You've taken the time to define what excellence looks like. If you want excellence, make sure that your actions, practices, and habit support what you seek. Table 6.1 offers a few common inconsistencies I've observed.

STEP 6

TABLE 6.1

Common Inconsistencies between What Managers Say Is Excellence and What Their Actions Communicate

What They Say	But What They Do
They value candor and diversity.	They become defensive when challenged or when people offer alternative ideas.
They want meetings to be productive and move work forward.	They facilitate ineffective meetings and book meetings that aren't viewed as a good use of time.
They value collaboration and teamwork.	They reward and reinforce only or primarily individual contributions.
They expect all employees to model the highest standards of professionalism.	They gossip and denigrate peer managers in front of team members.
They want the team to be change resilient and agile.	They resist changes that make them personally uncomfortable or require a lot of work.
They want the team to be customer focused and to provide excellent internal and external service.	They neglect to collect and/or listen to customer feedback or measure the team's performance based on customer-centric metrics.
They want the team to think creatively and generate ideas for improvement.	They don't support team members who want to get together to share and discuss ideas.

Think about the actions you took yesterday. How many of them support your vision of excellence? The more consistent your actions, the clearer your vision will become for all team members. Defining, communicating, and modeling a vision for excellence are powerful ways to ensure that your team is set up for success. It's tough to hit a target when you can see it, but nearly impossible when you can't.

It's also a great idea to bring Step 1 (clarify expectations of you), Step 2 (understand results you're expected to achieve), Step 3 (determine key department metrics), and Step 6 (define team excellence) together now. Do you see how the products of these steps combine to help you plan and run your piece of the business? The efforts you make in those steps also make great communication tools. Share your work from these steps with your manager and your team.

Tune Up and Realign Strategy for Step 6

STEP **6**

◆ Read the sample definition of excellence I provided in this step.
◆ Decide if you're able now to articulate your vision of excellence.
◆ Decide if each of your team members knows what extraordinary performance looks like? If not, take the time to draft a rough definition of excellence and share it with your team. Ask members to add to it and make suggestions for what needs to change.
◆ In one-on-one exchanges with your team members, make sure that each person understands how you'll evaluate excellence for her or his job. It's important to negotiate and calibrate your expectations of him or her and his or her expectations of you as the manager.

NOTES

_____

_____

_____

_____

_____

_____

_____

_____

_____

_____

_____

_____

_____

_____

_____

_____

_____

_____

_____

_____

_____

_____

Plan the Work and Work the Plan—Flexibly

Building a habit of planning

Sharing your plans

Encouraging your team to plan

Acting with perseverance and agility

Planning is critical, but it's a relatively rare activity. We can be more focused and successful if we spend just a few minutes planning each day. Most of the managers I've observed don't plan enough. They perceive it as not being fun, not being exciting, and—most important—not urgent. By definition, planning isn't something that has to be done right now. That makes it a perfect target for procrastination. Of course we all know that choosing to wait or skipping it entirely will only bite us in the butt later because today's urgent tasks probably are looming because we didn't plan in the past. It's a vicious circle—a time-sucking ride you can get off of by developing a regular practice of planning.

Before I share my thoughts on how to plan, I'd like to define what I mean by *planning*. Some people think they've planned if they've drafted a to-do list—and I guess that is planning at its lowest stage of efficacy. But you're not reading this book because you want to struggle along at a low level of productivity, right? You're using this book to help you blow the lid off your productivity and

POINTER

Planning helps you make better choices about how to spend your precious time

success. In other words—creating a to-do list isn't good enough to constitute your daily planning.

Planning is the combined efforts of thinking about the contribution that you and your team can make today (this week, this month, this year, this decade) and making specific choices about those actions that will best support your intentions. When you plan, keep both short-term and long-term goals in mind. To achieve long-term goals one day, work on them a wee bit each day along with shorter-term objectives.

Planning isn't boring and mundane—it's where managerial magic happens because it's where you make the decisions about how to spend your time and how to focus your team's energies, passions, and strengths. It's like going on a shopping spree with $5,000 in your hands—choosing what to buy is fun, but it's also important you choose wisely! Your time and your team's time are the $5,000 cash (and a lot more than that for some of you).

Building a Habit of Planning

How will you spend your $5,000? Will you blow it on short-term needs and wants, or invest in the future? Effective planning helps you and your team make the most of your impact on today's and tomorrow's results. To improve your planning practice, develop weekly and daily planning habits.

Weekly Habits

◆ Take 30 minutes on Friday afternoons or Monday mornings to plan for the upcoming week (adjust the timing if you work a different schedule). Think about the grand-slam home run described in Step 2 here again. What would represent grand-slam home run performance for the coming week (again, thinking about your short-term and long-term goals)? If you and your team excelled, what would occur? Ask your team for thoughts on this in a quick planning huddle (5–10 minutes).

◆ Schedule the meetings and conversations that will help you move things forward. Don't just write down, "Talk with Joe about the ABC project timeline"; schedule a meeting with Joe.

◆ Create a list of decisions you want to make or facilitate, and a list of barriers that need to be obliterated. Post the list where you'll refer to it daily.

◆ Think about coaching you can offer that would be most helpful to the team. Identify at least one skill or situation about which you'll seek coaching.

POINTER

Planning is thinking about the contributions that you and your team can make today and making specific choices about the best actions to support your intentions.

Daily Habits

◆ Spend 20 minutes planning at the beginning of each workday.

◆ Choose two or three actions you can take today that will make the greatest difference to your short-term and long-term goals. Take those actions.

◆ Take a few minutes to consider each team member's focus for the day. Is each person working on his or her most important projects or tasks? What adjustments should you make? What support or coaching would be most helpful? Is anyone up against a barrier you can obliterate so she or he can move forward?

◆ Take time at the beginning of each day to plan your meeting participation or leadership. Think about the value of the time each person spends sitting around the meeting room table. Meetings are expensive! When people come to meetings

STEP 7

POINTER

If you do just a little planning on a daily and weekly basis, you will significantly improve focus and results.

unprepared, they waste time and money. Set the standard and ensure your meetings are productive and move work forward.

The weekly planning habits become the foundation for your daily planning. Trust me on this—the process works. Try the weekly and daily planning habits for one month. You'll feel on top of your work and you'll be getting much more accomplished.

Worksheets 7.1 and 7.2 offer easy-to-use checklist forms to make these practices habitual and permanent parts of your managerial regimen. Give these worksheets a try for a couple weeks, and I promise you'll feel more in control and on top of your busy day.

It feels great to go home after a long day and feel like you actually accomplished something. Without effective planning, you'll be more likely to get sucked into issues and diversions that you might regret later.

Sharing Your Plans and Spreading the Practice

STEP **7**

If you do the weekly and daily planning and then follow your plans, you'll be more productive—I guarantee it. If you share your plans and your planning regimen in a way that inspires your team members and peers to try planning as well, your planning will have an even greater impact. Sharing the plan helps improve clarity and commitment. People understand what's most important and your focus for the day and week. Getting your team members interesting in building their planning muscles multiplies the benefits to be gained.

I'm a big fan of the huddle for communicating the weekly and daily focus. I don't like to create a bunch of meetings where people take too much time to go around and say what they're doing. That's a waste of time. The huddle, on the other hand, is a short, focused,

WORKSHEET 7.1

Weekly Planning Checklist

Instructions: Use this planning checklist to set aside time and energy for the most important work tasks. Start by defining a grand-slam home run goal for the week (an accomplishment that would make a significant positive impact on the department, project, and/or company). Write down two to four items for the other planning elements and then use this information to plan your week. Review and revise this worksheet daily or as needed.

Planning Element	Your Plan for the Week
Gland-slam home run *for the week:*	
Meetings and conversations I need to schedule	
Decisions needed, and by whom	
Coaching and developing for the week	
Any *must-not-miss* items	
Potential barriers to hitting the grand slam for the week	

STEP **7**

WORKSHEET 7.2

Daily Planning Checklist

Instructions: Transfer your weekly grand-slam home run goal from the weekly planning worksheet. At the beginning of each day, take 10 minutes to define the actions you intend to take for each planning element. Carry this checklist with you to meetings and review it midday to ensure you're on track and focused on the right work.

Planning Element	Your Plan for the Day
Gland-slam home run for the week (transfer from weekly checklist):	
Two or three actions I can take today that will make the greatest difference	
Team focus—any adjustments to be made	
Barriers I need to obliterate	
Meetings and preparation needed	

stand-up meeting that accomplishes a lot in a little time. Don't sit—it will lengthen the huddle. If everyone knows they'll huddle for 10 minutes at 9:30 each morning and that each person is expected to share the plan for the day, individual plans will be made before 9:30. This practice promotes good planning.

Worksheet 7.3 offers a format you can use to post the team's daily plan on a whiteboard or flipchart. If you use a whiteboard, you can create the checklist form with black tape and easily add to and erase daily information.

Some of you may be thinking that this sounds a bit like micromanagement. Daily planning and daily huddles shouldn't look or feel like that. In fact, when done well, these habits encourage ownership and independence among members of the team. Why do so many managers micromanage? Because they don't have effective communication practices, and they feel uncomfortable not knowing what's going on within the team. Huddling builds awareness and a shared understanding of priorities, but it's never long enough to become a device for micromanagement.

POINTER

A great way to share daily plans is with brief morning team huddles.

STEP 7

Another potential objection you may have is that holding morning huddles gives the manager too much information from which to micromanage later in the day. If you're a micromanager (offering more direction and control than is warranted to maximize productivity), the information offered in a huddle may be grist for your mill. Here's the simple solution—just don't grind it that way.

I believe the huddle offers managers a good look at what the team is focusing on and which tasks will be accomplished each day. If a team member isn't working on the right things, it's a great opportunity for you to help get his or her work on track. We all want our efforts to be focused and worthwhile, so this kind of refocusing should be welcome—not seen as picayune meddling.

WORKSHEET 7.3

Daily Team Planning Checklist

Instructions: Write the names of your team members in the left-hand column. Ask each team member to share his or her top two priorities for the day at a morning huddle or informal check-in. Write the priorities in the right-hand column. Refer to this checklist during meetings and informal conversations throughout the day.

Team Member	Top Two Priorities for the Day

Acting with Perseverance and Agility

Your weekly and daily planning habits help you and your team steer in the right direction. You've heard the saying, "Plan your work, then work your plan," right? I agree with that wholeheartedly— with one addition. Plan your work and work your plan *unless your plan needs to change.* To optimize your productivity and impact, be relentless in working your plan while being nimble in case things need to change.

Here's a true story. To a senior leadership team, I presented a plan that had several recommendations. The team adopted some of the recommendations and rejected some others. The CEO was uncomfortable with changing certain aspects of the product even though the rest of the folks sitting around the table thought the product was getting dusty and needed to change. I was asked after the meeting if I felt my efforts were wasted because some recommendations weren't adopted. I know there are people who would have answered "yes," but my view is different. I believe that, as managers, we're here to make a difference. It's always our job to prepare and share recommendations about how we think we can improve the business. That said, we have to go where the energy is. To have an impact, we need to get things done. Instead of digging our heels in and becoming stubborn, it's much more effective to move full-steam ahead where we can and make adjustments. It's more important that we *have* an impact on the business than that we get there in precisely the ways we planned.

Similarly, it's important not to get too attached to a plan or a project. As I've shared with you a few times earlier in this book, many departments continue to work on projects that should have been killed. Make sure yours is isn't one of those departments. It's good to review your task and project list once a month, and to ask yourself and your team if these items still make sense, given the current priorities and what you think they'll be in the future. It feels wonderful—liberating—to kill a project when it ought to be killed. Think of all the time and energy you've saved by putting it out of *your* misery! You just put your $5,000 back in the bank and available for other pursuits.

What about yearly planning? I'm not addressing it in this book, but your daily planning ought to flow from the yearly or quarterly goals you set as part of the budgeting and planning cycle. When you do the weekly planning, I assume that you're working from your departmental business plan or the goals you negotiated with your manager. That said, most of those goals will not be expressed in terms of grand-slam home runs, so you'll want to make those distinctions and additions.

Here's an idea: Share the concept of grand-slam home runs with your peers and manager, and recommend that you create yearly goals with that level of excellence in mind. Oh no, are you rolling your eyes at me? OK, start with your area and expand after you've had some success using grand-slam goals.

Plan the work, work the plan, and make adjustments. Zoom forward!

Tune Up and Realign Strategy for Step 7

STEP 7

- ◆ Try using the weekly and daily planning worksheets for two weeks. Then modify the practices to fit your style and needs.
- ◆ Review your project and task list, making sure you don't have any items that need to come off the list. If you find any, *do* take them off.
- ◆ Try the team huddle for two weeks. It takes a week or so for people to get into the groove and pace of the meeting. You'll find after a week that the huddles will be short and very sweet.

STEP **7**

STEP **7**

Obliterate Barriers

Obliterating barriers is almost a religious experience. Managers who see this as part of their calling know that getting rid of barriers can be a huge rush and thrill. Really, I'm not kidding. Although some managers avoid conflict, complexity, and complication, others search for them like a heat-seeking missile zooms to its target. To be a better manager, you'll want to be a champion barrier obliterator.

In the first management book I wrote, *High Impact Middle Management: Solutions for Today's Busy Managers* (Adams Media 2005), I called barriers "mucky muck." I still like that very descriptive term so I'll continue using it here. Mucky muck is all the goo and gunk that gets in your way and in your team members' ways each day. Mucky muck might be redundant tasks, politics inhibiting candid conversation, broken processes, backlogs, bad or missing information, or delays (figure 8.1). Every organization has its share of mucky muck and its own brand of barriers.

One company I worked with was thick with unspoken procedures and practices. In meetings, everyone nodded their heads in

STEP **8**

FIGURE 8.1

How Mucky Muck Forms a Production Barrier

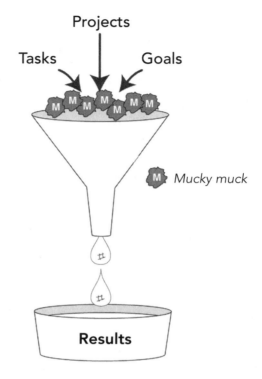

Projects

Tasks   Goals

M *Mucky muck*

Results

agreement with proposed changes; but then they'd leave the room and nothing would change. People said they agreed with an idea but they knew it was useless to talk about because the CEO would never go for it. When recruiting for managers, they said they wanted someone to shake things up, but really they wanted people who wouldn't make waves. Their unspoken hopes and expectations ran the place, and new managers very quickly had to learn what was not being said so they could have an impact (and not go insane).

Another organization I worked for repelled any kind of structure or organization. It prided itself on being hip, fast-paced, and

STEP **8**

innovative. They were thick with the mucky muck of redundancy, miscommunication, and disorganization. Managers who helped bridge that gap and provided their teams with some consistent communication made working at this company more satisfying and fruitful. Whatever the types of mucky muck you have at your company, it's your job to obliterate as much as you can—that's why you're there.

POINTER

Obliterating barriers is an important (and fun) part of every manager's job.

Building Your Obliteration Muscles

Would you like to know how to become a champion barrier obliterator? Practice, practice, practice. You need to learn to see mucky muck for what it is, then act in ways that will scrub the highest amount away from your team. Here are some of the ways that you can build your barrier obliteration muscles:

◆ **Start seeing things in terms of processes.** What's the decision-making process? What's the project management process? What's the process for getting data and reports? Once you see the process in play, look for what's slowing down any aspect of the process. Where does information get stuck? Which steps of the process cause the most trouble? When you start seeing processes and how the work flows, you also can see where it stops—and that's where you're likely to find mucky muck.

◆ **Notice how certain people respond to certain questions and comments.** We all have triggers that enliven action or make us defensive. Champion barrier obliterators learn how to communicate to create the greatest likelihood of cooperation and partnership from others. You need to learn people's preferences and communication styles to maximize your influence.

◆ **Ask your peers and team members what's hindering them.** Ask often because you want to create a dialogue that ensures they'll share barriers with you as soon as they

STEP 8

encounter them. It's easier to get rid of new mucky muck than it is to rid the organization of a years-old problem. The practice of asking also will help you be more proactive if your natural tendency is to avoid conflict and complication.

◆ **Start with yourself.** Obliterate the barriers standing in your way. Clean a path so you can spend more time supporting others. What are the barriers in your way? Disorganization, miscommunication with a peer, decisions needed from your manager, attendance at too many useless meetings? Fix these things, and then move on to other sources of mucky muck.

All organizations have lots of mucky muck, so you'll have many opportunities to exercise those obliteration muscles—your "oblits." Table 8.1 suggests some times ripe for a good workout.

TABLE 8.1

Conditions Ripe for Practicing Barrier Obliteration

When	What to Look For
Team meetings	Notice energy-level drops and nonverbal communication. If people seem frustrated or concerned, they may be dealing with mucky muck.
Your staff meetings with peers	Notice the people or topics that provoke resistance. What's going on and how might you help?
Project reviews	Notice the constraints and steps along the process that are slow or stalled. Which process steps cause the most delay and frustration?
Requests you need to repeat	If you make a request and the person does not complete the request, he or she is likely dealing with some kind of barrier.
Things that make your eyes roll	Pay attention to your own body language. Instead of putting up with frustration and red tape again and again, fix it!
Water-cooler complaints	Listen to what people are talking about. Their complaints often are caused by mucky muck.

Approach each day with barrier obliteration in mind. We see what we look for, and we're blind to that which we ignore. If we wait for barriers to knock at the office door, we'll miss most of them or get to them when it's too late to prevent problems. Some people look in the desert and see only sand—others can tell it's teeming with life. Your organization is alive with mucky muck. Look for it!

Identifying and Getting Rid of Barriers

POINTER Get rid of the mucky muck standing in your way so you're better able to help remove obstacles that your team is facing.

Your team members are relying on you to cut through the mucky muck and help them get their jobs done. Although it's important to choose your battles, getting rid of mucky muck is often one of the best ways you can spend your valuable time. That said, focus on getting rid of the most problematic barriers first. Here are a few strategies for identifying and getting rid of barriers:

◆ **Overcommunicate.** Make sure your team understands that you want to know what's getting in the way of its ability to do its best work. Share any relevant information you have because a lack of information is a very common source of mucky muck. (Don't be a mucky muck generator by keeping information to yourself.)

◆ **Do some analysis.** Find out what's causing the problem and fix it. Take the initiative to dig into the data or files to determine the root cause. Or, better yet, encourage and support team members who want to take the time to do the analysis.

◆ **Ask better questions.** Mucky muck often results from poor communication somewhere down the line. Ask probing questions to engage people in open and candid conversation about the barrier. Try to determine the intent and reduce the power of unproductive motives and hidden agendas.

◆ **Fix strained relationships.** A common barrier is formed when two or more people don't communicate enough with

STEP **8**

each other because their relationship is strained or has suffered a setback. It's important to fix dysfunctional relationships. Be the bigger person (or help your team member be so) who approaches the other person and extends the olive branch. Share your regrets about the situation and apologize for your part in the breakdown. (You did play a part, whether you were directly involved in the situation or served as the manager of those involved.)

◆ **Never give up.** Don't lose faith in people's capacity to change. Sometimes timing makes the difference, and sometimes it's the way the subject is communicated that affects how and whether a person will react.

◆ **Lighten up and roll with it.** Every company has mucky muck. Think of it as job security!

Enjoy your role as a barrier obliterator. When you get rid of workplace hassles, you make things better for everyone. It's also important to acknowledge and prepare for the fact that your work will never be over. Barriers will keep rising. This isn't a part of your job that you can conquer once and be done with it. Barrier obliteration is a lifelong part of management. Oh, yeah!

Building an Environment of Barrier Obliteration

As a champion barrier obliterator, you'll be the most popular manager on your floor, if not in the whole company. Why not spread that energy and create teams of barrier obliterators? You can create an environment where barriers are quickly identified and removed if you encourage open dialogue and curious investigation. Reinforce open group discussions about mucky muck and help coach team members on ways they can remove the obstacles getting in their way. Support team members when they want to create ad hoc project teams to quickly investigate and remove barriers and constraints.

Creating an environment where barriers are proactively obliterated by all team members takes some strength, courage, and matu-

STEP
8

rity. You and your team members need to be open to productive criticism and challenge. After all, a lot of the mucky muck will be generated within the department. In addition, together you will need to develop ways to influence other departments to cooperate in removing obstacles within their control or jurisdiction. Underpinning this environment is open and trusting communication supported by deep work relationships.

There I go again, writing about the importance of profound interpersonal connections. Well, it's true. We're more willing to take direct and potentially painful feedback from someone we know and believe cares about us than we are to accept it from a team member with whom we have a relationship based on politeness or competitiveness.

Tune Up and Realign Strategy for Step 8

◆ At you next team meeting, go around the table and ask each person to list the top three things keeping her or him from doing the best possible work. Then ask the team to enumerate barriers that are getting in the way of the entire team. Add your barriers to the list. The result is your barrier seed list.

◆ Ask questions that help you understand the extent to which each barrier is a problem for an individual or the team as a whole.

◆ Prioritize the list by defining each item's impact if removed and enumerating the resources needed to remove each barrier.

◆ Tackle one or two barriers each day.

◆ Refresh the list by asking your team the same questions every two months or as needed.

STEP **8**

STEP **8**

Proactively Manage Change and Transition

OVERVIEW

Learning how people transition

Managing your ability to transition

Helping others transition

Change is the only constant. You'll face more changes in the next year than you have in the last three years. Blah, blah, blah. You read that there is and will be lots of change. You don't need me to tell you about it. There is a management challenge however, because I know of very few managers who manage change well. This is important because when you and your team members fail to transition, lots of problems get worse. Stack more changes on top of that situation, and the work environment will look and feel very chaotic. This is when people start to burn out and leave.

You know there's change, but do you know how to help your people get through it? If you've read any of my other books, you may think this step reads like a broken record. Whenever *change* is the topic, I share the Bridges Transition Model and I'm going to do it here again because it's a terrifically effective tool for managers who need to help people through changes. It's actually my favorite change management model.

Change is very important, but most companies—and most managers—don't invest the time and attention required to ensure that

POINTER

Situations change and people transition. Transition is the internal process people go through when they react to and adjust to changes.

employees transition well. That's a shame because managing transitions isn't rocket science. In fact, when you understand the nature of transition, it's relatively easy to do. In 1991, William Bridges published an important book, titled *Managing Transitions: Making the Most of Change* (Perseus Books), that addressed how people respond to change. You should not implement a change without considering the process people go through to transition. There are other models of personal transition, but the Bridges Transition Model is the most comprehensive one, and it has stood the test of time. According to Bridges, *change* and *transition* are not the same thing. Change is a situation where something transforms: Jobs are added/eliminated, the company merges with a competitor, health benefits decrease/increase, new software is loaded, regulatory requirements increase, or the company reorganizes.

Transition is the inner process through which people come to terms with a change. Transition is the path people have to take to react to and get comfortable with change. The process includes letting go of the way things used to be and growing more at ease with the way things are now. Transition is personal. Each individual will transition at a different speed and in a different way in reaction to various changes. In an organization, managing transition means helping people make this process less painful and troublesome. Changes are external transitions are internal.

To manage a change successfully, managers need to understand and take into account how people transition.

Learning How People Transition

Here's a summary of the Bridges Transition Model, adapted from a book I wrote titled *Organization Development Basics* (ASTD Press 2005).

FIGURE 9.1

Phases of the Bridges Transition Model

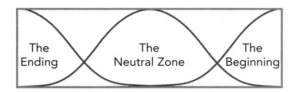

| The Ending | The Neutral Zone | The Beginning |

Bridges Transition Model

Transition occurs in three phases: ending, the neutral zone, and new beginning. Figure 9.1 shows how these phases flow and overlap.

Phase 1: Ending

Every transition begins with an ending, a loss. When things change, employees leave behind the way things used to be. They're left searching for a new way to define their reality. Even if the change is perceived as positive, there's some loss and something that's ending. Before you can transition to a new beginning, you must let go of the way that things used to be.

Sometimes people resist giving up ways and practices that have made them successful in the past. They're reluctant to give up what feels right and comfortable.

Phase 2: The Neutral Zone

The neutral zone is a confusing in-between state in which people are on their way to the new beginning. They're no longer in the past, but haven't yet reached the new beginning. It's that ambiguous place in the middle that feels murky and ill defined. They may feel lost. For some, the neutral zone is so full of confusion that getting through it drains their energies. People are so driven to get out of the neutral zone that some rush ahead while others retreat into the past. Neither of those approaches is advisable because the neutral zone has a purpose.

Although this zone can be confusing or distressing, it also can be a very creative place. Time in the neutral zone isn't wasted because this is where the real transformation takes place. The external change can continue forward on something close to its own schedule while the internal transition is being attended to; but if the transition isn't dealt with, the change may collapse. People can't do the new things that the new situation requires until they come to grips with what is being asked of them.

POINTER

Time spent in the neutral zone can be very creative. Take the time to engage your team in creative new ways to get to the new beginning. There are many paths to the goal.

Phase 3: New Beginning

A new beginning can happen only after people have let go of the past and spent some time in the neutral zone. In this third phase, people accept the reality of the change and start to identify with their new situation.

Some people fail to get through transition because they don't let go of the old ways and make an ending; others fail because they become frightened and confused by the uncertainty of the neutral zone and don't stay in it long enough for it to do its work on them. Some people get through those first two phases of transition, but freeze when they face the third phase, the new beginning. This phase requires people to behave in a new way, and that can be worrisome because it tests one's competence and confidence. Employees will hang back during the final phase of transition if the organization has been known to punish people for mistakes. They'll wait to see how others handle the new beginning before they jump in.

Tool 9.1 describes possible behaviors that you might see in each transition phase. A person may display one, more than one, or none of the behaviors, but these are the most common and likely ones.

TOOL 9.1

Typical Transition Behaviors

Transition Phase	Behavior You May See
Phase 1: Ending	Avoidance, clinging to the old, going through the motions, disbelief, shock, anger, mistakes, sabotage, carelessness
Phase 2: Neutral zone	Detachment, withdrawal, confusion, lack of attentiveness, mood swings, indifference, creativity, risk taking, experimentation, participation
Phase 3: New beginning	Behavior consistent with the change, focus on purpose, renewed energy, clarity of role, feeling of competence

Managing Your Ability to Transition

You've probably seen the safety video on airplane flights—the one in which they tell you, in the event of a loss of cabin pressurization, to put your oxygen mask on first before trying to help a child or someone else. I know many parents who would say that's rubbish and who'd help their children first. When it comes to organizational transition, it *is* important that you put your oxygen mask on first, and then help your team members. You're going to be a lousy leader of change if you're struggling to transition. We can't be stuck and helping others move forward at the same time.

Take a look at the techniques for helping others transition that I've listed in the next section. You can apply those same techniques to help yourself transition. Here are some examples:

- Define what's changing for you. What is ending and what are you losing. Mark the ending.
- Make sure you're clear about your part in the transition. Talk to your manager and share your questions and concerns.
- Be patient with yourself, and expect that you might have a range of emotions and reactions. This is fine; we all transition in different ways and at differing speeds.

STEP **9**

The Marathon Effect

Think about a marathon. There are thousands of people bunched up behind the starting line. The start gun blasts and the folks in the front begin to run. Then slowly the people behind them start to run, and it takes several minutes before the people who were in the back of the line can begin moving. As the race proceeds, the running pack thins out and runners come across the finish line a few at a time over a period of hours.

Transition is similar. The folks planning the change (usually management) start their transition days, weeks, or months ahead of the rest of the organization. By the time the change is rolled out, the managers have crossed the transition finish line (new beginnings). But the other folks are only starting their transition, and they won't all run at the same pace. Some will need extra support and a few may not make it across the finish line at all. It's important you grasp the marathon effect to understand how people might be feeling so you can show empathy and support for those who are just then being thrust into endings.

◆ Set realistic goals for yourself and celebrate successes—even small ones!

If you find that you're struggling with a change, talk to your manager or a trusted peer. Do whatever it takes to make the transition, and then help your team members.

Helping Others Transition

You have a huge opportunity to help your team members, peers, and even your manager (coaching up!) transition to changes. Here are a few strategies to use for each phase of the transition.

Planning Strategies (Before the Change Is Implemented)

◆ Talk about transition with your team. Share the Bridges model so members can help you help others transition, and can be more aware of their personal reactions.

- Be clear with people about what is ending—from your perspective and their points of view. Identify what they'll lose and how behaviors and attitudes will need to change.
- Plan and schedule communications. Be sure you plan for lots of communication carried on in a variety of ways, including announcement meetings, smaller discussion meetings, daily briefings, handouts, and managing by walking around.

POINTER

Managers need to ensure they transition well before they can manage change effectively or help others transition.

Ending Strategies

- Communicate, communicate, and communicate. Err on the side of too much communication. Explain the need for the change and why the change makes sense now. Communicate the 4Ps: What's the picture? What's the purpose? What's the plan? What's my part? Define and communicate what is and is not changing.

4 Ps

- Mark the ending. One of the reasons people get stuck in the ending phase is that they don't acknowledge what's ending; they hang on to the old ways. Mark the ending in a respectful and clear way. Openly acknowledge losses.
- Don't be blindsided by people who seem to overreact. Everyone's transition is different, so ensure that you're ready to experience a wide variety of responses.

Neutral Zone Strategies

- Continue to communicate the 4Ps.
- Create temporary systems, roles, policies, and processes to help normalize the neutral zone.
- Set realistic productivity targets, and expect some slowdowns.
- Provide training and development to help raise competence and maintain confidence.

STEP 9

- Encourage people to share ideas and participate in refining the details of the change. The neutral zone can be a very creative time, and you want to take advantage of that. Encourage experimentation and idea brainstorming.
- Get people involved in the change plan and working together to make the change seem less isolating.

New Beginning Strategies

- Continue to communicate the 4Ps. Ensure that you communicate often and with consistency. Be open about setbacks and challenges and enlist people to be part of the solution.
- Celebrate successes, even small ones. Reward people for making the transition.
- Ensure that temporary policies and structures are replaced with ones that are consistent with the new situation.
- Reflect on the change and the transitions that people have made. Measure the effectiveness of the change process and identify any outstanding action items.

POINTER

To help facilitate acceptance of changes, frequently communicate the 4Ps: What's the picture? What's the purpose? What's the plan? What's my part?

When in doubt, share the model and communicate the 4Ps! If people don't transition successfully, they can't perform well. Transition is a team competency that, once developed, will serve you and your team through the many changes to come.

STEP 9

Tune Up and Realign Strategy for Step 9

- Use the Bridges Transition Model to help you plan for and manage your next change.
- Share the model with your team, and create communication strategies that will help you facilitate transition.

◆ Talk openly with your team members about the phases of transition, and remember that each person may transition differently.

◆ I recommend that you read William Bridges' book *Managing Transitions*. There's an exercise in the book that management teams should do together before implementing any large change initiatives.

NOTES

STEP **9**

STEP
9

Leave a Legacy of Capacity to Produce

Management is sometimes a thankless, stressful, and difficult profession. Most of us don't do this kind of work for the money or the fame, and we often get neither. We manage because we want to make a big difference. We step up and into the mucky muck because we know we can leave things looking, sounding, and feeling better than when we took over as manager. That's the vision that ties together millions of dedicated managers. I love working with managers because they're the engines of the organization. If the engine starts running 10 percent better, the effect is amazing. All managers want to make a difference. The particular shape of that impact is your legacy. When you leave the job or company, what mark do you want to leave behind?

Let's do a little reality check here. How many of you have taken over a new job and found that your predecessor left the department in a shambles? Roles are unclear, people are fried, and projects aren't getting done on time. That happens a lot—and not just when a manager is terminated. Why do many talented and smart managers leave a mess for the next person?

Let's think about why people leave jobs. Many of the managers I know who have left their jobs when they were burned out and couldn't take it any longer. We rarely leave jobs at the height of our effectiveness, but I'd like to propose that you do. Unless you're about to have a stress-induced heart attack or something else dire, make sure you leave your department looking and feeling great. Instead of short-timer's disease (becoming a lame duck during your last two weeks), try setting a new standard in leaving well. It feels great to go out that way.

POINTER

All managers should think about the legacy they wish to leave. Creating a legacy vision will help shape your actions and results today and in the future.

Visualizing Your Legacy

What kind of a legacy would you like to leave? Is there a particular project for which you want to be known? Would you like to create an amazing team? Do you want to revolutionize the way your company plans for innovation? Do you want to lead record-breaking gains in financial performance? Imagine that you're a fly in the elevator one week after you leave. Two people are talking about you. What is it you want them to say?

In addition to the broad or grand accomplishments you seek, think about the ways in which you want to be known as a role model. Do you want to be remembered as the queen of exciting meetings? (That would be my goal.) Or the king of provocative analysis? Do you want to be known as always organized and prepared? Creative and innovative? Fun? Think about how you want to be known and the type of reputation you want to build. Write down your rough thoughts on Worksheet 10.1.

Can you visualize your legacy—see it come to fruition? Notice the details of how success looks, and include those details in your weekly and daily planning regimen (Step 7). Spend three to four minutes every morning and every afternoon visualizing the legacy

STEP 10

WORKSHEET 10.1

Creating Your Legacy Vision

Instructions: Think about the legacy you want to leave for each of the aspects of management listed in the left-hand column. Write your legacy goals for each aspect of management in the spaces provided in the right-hand column.

Aspects of Management	The Legacy You Want to Leave
Results and contribution to the business	
Team health and development	
Peer partnership and collaboration	
Creativity and innovation	
Processes and practices	
Workplace culture	
Systems and structure	
Change and agility	

STEP
10

111

you want to leave. Repeated visualization is a powerful tool that will seep into your daily choices, actions, and conversations.

Being What You Seek

That headline is inspired by one of my all-time-favorite quotes from Mahatma Gandhi: "You must be the change you wish to see in the world." I believe that's true and I remind myself of it often when I'm dissatisfied with a result.

You're leaving your legacy today—the question is, are you leaving the legacy you want to leave? If you want to be known for helping turn the department around, start turning it around today. If you want to be known for being prepared and organized, be that today.

POINTER

A great way to ensure your management legacy is to act today in alignment with the change you seek.

Being it today doesn't mean that we've arrived at the final level of performance; it means that who we are being is consistent with our goals. A really clear way to describe this is to use the example of diet and fitness. Let's say you are 50 pounds overweight and inactive. Your goals are to be vibrant and healthy and, one day, to run a marathon. You can't run a marathon today and you shouldn't try, but you can behave in a way that is consistent with being vibrant, healthy, and a runner:

- ◆ **Consistent:** Eat lots of fruits, vegetables, whole grains, and lean protein; walk two miles; do 20 minutes of weight training; finish the evening with 20 minutes of yoga stretching and relaxation.
- ◆ **Not consistent:** Say you'll exercise tomorrow; have a cheeseburger, fries, and cola for lunch three days in a row; think about what you'll eat differently tomorrow.

Do you see the distinction? Sure, everyone has to have a cheeseburger every now and then, but, on balance, are you being the change you seek to make in this world/your company? I once worked alongside and coached a pal. He wanted to leave a legacy of a strong and collaborative leadership team. The problem was that his style was sometimes too provocative, pushy, and intense. He was the biggest barrier to the team's collaboration. On days when he remembered that, he was able to be consistent with his goal and to modify his approach to build conversation and collaboration. The best way to ensure that you leave the legacy you seek is to start being it today.

POINTER

Show the organization how to leave with style and grace—leave your department and office in better shape than you received it.

Leaving Things in Better Shape

Here's a pet peeve of mine: I start a new job, get into my new office, look around, check out the desk and file cabinets—and there's junk everywhere! Unused ketchup packets in the top right-hand drawer, tons of stuff filling the in-box, and what looks like an open bag of roasted peanuts in the top drawer commingling with 85 half-used pens, 23 bitten-on pencils, and 13 bottles of dried-up White-Out. How many of you have started a new job and had this same experience? How many of you have left offices in this shape? Come on, be honest! Please don't do this to the next person. Leave your workspace in great condition—better than when you got it. I bet some people never bother to clean out the peanuts and end up passing them on to manager after manager after manager, like a Christmas fruit cake.

Show pride in the work you've done, and help pave the way for the next person's success. Even if you're leaving because you can't stand the job any longer, take the high road.

My example only went so far as to describe the desk (but it's an excellent visual, no?). You need to do the same with projects, initiatives, personnel challenges, and incomplete tasks. Leave them all in better shape than when you took over the job. I once took over a job and the woman before me did not even take the time to delete her personal emails. Her emails were transferred to me so that I would have the vendor contacts, but I also got lots of creepy messages about her dates and shopping habits—yuck! That's just plain lazy and, in these days of enhanced access, dangerous because you never know what's going to end up on some blog or written in a management book as a "don't do this," example. Take the last two weeks to clean things up in general and have fun going out with a glorious bang.

Start living your legacy today, even though you may not leave this job for years. Improve the team's strength and capacity. Improve processes. Be the fullest expression of your unique self and give your organization the very best you have to offer. Establish a better process for managing new projects. Teach the organization how to have fun and get a lot done.

Tune Up and Realign Strategy for Step 10

- Do you know the legacy you want to leave as a manager? The time to start thinking about that is now, not six months before you leave the company.
- Things change and you'll change. Take some time to think about the impact you want to have and how you can best act in alignment with that vision today.
- Think about your legacy when you do your weekly and daily planning.

CONCLUSION

There you have it—my 10 steps to better management. Are they the only steps? No. Are they sequential steps? They don't have to be. Are they really steps at all? Who knows—it depends on how you look at them. All that being the case, here's something I wholeheartedly believe: If you try the techniques suggested in those 10 steps, you'll have a more fruitful and enjoyable career as a manager.

I've been a manager for many years and surely will hold management roles again in the future. What I've described in the 10 steps are the techniques that I've seen work for others and that have worked for me.

Oh, there's one more step. Well, it's not really a step, but it's something important to mention. If you're going to be a manager and you're going to dedicate your career to one of the toughest and most vital jobs there is (remember, you're the engine!), then it's *critical* that you have fun.

Do you let your job suck you into its vortex of tasks, reports, emails, and stacks of reading material? Having fun and doing great work are complementary—you can and should do both. It's fun to be focused and moving forward; and when we have fun, we have more energy for our work. Fun is different for each person. You don't have to explode in extroverted joy at the sight of the office supply delivery. Just make sure that you enjoy your work and that your pleasure shows in the way you show joy. As the manager, you need to model a focus on fun and to encourage your team members to have fun, too. If you honestly don't find your work to be fun, change your job. Life's too short to toil away at work that gives you no pleasure or satisfaction.

Fun = pleasure. Pleasure is a feeling of happy satisfaction and enjoyment. It comes from the positive, and if you have a positive outlook and express optimism for the future, you'll go a long way toward creating an attractive work environment. And it's infectious! When you infuse the work environment with positive energy and a caring spirit, you set the tone for all the other relationships in your area. Be fun and show optimism. (Are we on Step 12 now?).

You have to have fun and you must be likable (is this Step 13?). If you want to be a successful manager, being likable is no longer an option. Whether you're an introvert or an extrovert, you can and should be a pleasure to work with. Do your team members say, "Hey, I really like working with her," meaning you? If not, you've got some work to do. This is a serious management strategy, not just some fluff that makes work more pleasant. It's possible to be a jerk *and* get work out of people—but probably not more than about 50 percent of their potential.

Giving passion, heart, and soul to one's work is an option, a choice. Team members choose how much of themselves to give, based on how they feel about the work, the work environment, the company, and you. If you're a joy to work with, people will work harder for you—period. Everyone can be likable, *everyone*. Just like everyone has the potential to be annoying and a pain in the neck.

I've coached a few jerks, and I've had to share with them the perception that people had of them. You know what the common response was? "They don't know me. If they really knew me, they wouldn't hate me." This is often true—and it's their responsibility to make themselves known. I don't let managers off the hook easily when they have not taken the time to let their peers and team members get to know who they are, warts and all. Everyone has weird habits and personality flaws, but it's our flaws that make us interesting.

The easiest thing you can do to become more likable is to let people get to know you. Why do you do this work? What are your goals? Which moments of the day do you most enjoy/dislike? What are your hot buttons—those silly little things that cause a big reaction? What concerns keep you up at night? If you were given a six-month paid sabbatical, what would you do? Share stuff like that. Let people get to know you, and take the initiative to get to know them. People who have productive relationships enjoy working together. You and your team don't need to go bowling together, just take the time and make the effort to get to know one another.

Be likable and relax (Step 14?). Relate and relax. Try not to take things so seriously. I knew a manager who had a big and dramatic reaction to everything. He blew little issues and opportunities way out of proportion. He took his job and the work far too seriously, and he stressed out everyone around him. He could be a likable guy, but he oozed anxiety and nobody wanted to work with him. Unless you're the secretary-general of the United Nations or an emergency room trauma doctor, I'm sure you can relax more.

Management is a customer service job. To provide good service we need to relax and do unto others (Step 15?). I bet you think I'm going to write "do unto others as you want others to do unto you." I guess you're right because I just wrote it, but that's not the point I'm making here. My point is simpler: *Do unto others.* Help people out. Do nice things for people. Be thoughtful. Take the time to be a nice person. When you do your daily planning (Step 7), ask yourself what you can do for someone today, and then do that.

It's altruistically selfish to be nice to others! If you're nice and helpful, your peers and employees will come to your aid when you need it most. Imagine you just made a huge mistake and put the progress of a product launch on hold. Imagine that you need an extraordinary effort from everyone on the team to help you turn the situation around and get the product launch back on track. Now imagine you're in this situation and you haven't paid any attention to your team members. You haven't been particularly nice or helpful because you've been so self-absorbed with personal priorities. You're in a bit of trouble. Now picture it differently: You're a beloved manager who always goes out of his or her way to help others and show care. Your problem is solved.

OK, that's it, that's all you have to do to be a great manager.

People who want to manage—you know, people like you—are amazing, and I have nothing but respect and admiration for you all. As a trainer, coach, and fellow manager, I'm always interested in learning about the techniques that work best for you. Please consider dropping me an email with your feedback, ideas, and stories. You can find my current email address and a link to my management blog on my website, www.lisahaneberg.com.

So here's to great success and a grand management legacy!

I N D E X

teams, *continued*
    purpose of, 48–49
    types of, 45–46
transitions
    behaviors of, 102–3
    change vs., 100
    communication of, 105–7
    of employees, 100–103
    management of, 103–4

    planning for, 104–6
    techniques for, 103–6

V

visions, 110, 112, 114

W

workplace environments, 113–14

Lisa Haneberg is an expert in the areas of management, leadership, and personal and organizational success. She consults on organization development, management and leadership training, and human resources. Haneberg also offers integrated training solutions and individual and group coaching services. Her presentations on a range of leadership and management topics are enthusiastic and fun.

Her first book, *High Impact Middle Management: Solutions for Today's Busy Managers* (Adams Media 2005), was a groundbreaking read for professional middle managers. She also has written *Focus Like a Laser Beam: Ten Ways to Do What Matters Most* (Jossey-Bass 2006), *Two Weeks to a Breakthrough: How to Zoom Toward Your Goals in 14 Days or Less* (Jossey-Bass 2007), *Organization Development Basics* (ASTD Press 2005), and *Coaching Basics* (ASTD Press 2006). Haneberg reaches a worldwide audience through her popular management blog, "Management Craft" (www.managementcraft.com and www.allbusiness.com), which offers resources and perspectives to leaders and managers, and to those who develop and coach them. Her main website, www.haneberg-management.com, highlights her products and services.

Over the past 22 years, Haneberg has worked with leaders at all levels and for many types and sizes of organizations, including high-tech manufacturing (Intel); distribution, manufacturing, and services (Black & Decker, Mead Paper, Corbis); e-retailing and distribution (Amazon.com); travel and leisure products and services

(Beacon Hotel, Travcoa, and Cruise West); and the Royal Government of Thailand.

She earned an undergraduate degree in behavioral sciences from the University of Maryland, and has taken graduate courses at Johns Hopkins University, Ohio State University, and Goddard College. She lives in the beautiful Pacific Northwest with her husband, four dogs, and a cat; and, among other pursuits, she loves driving her motorcycle down winding roads.

10 Steps to Be a Successful Manager: Facilitator's Guide

Lisa Haneberg

Get off the "no-progress treadmill" and make the most of the *10 Steps to Be a Successful Manager* by putting them into action now. This companion facilitator's guide offers trainers, coaches, and other training professionals the structure they need to create great management training that gets results. Rather than a traditional workbook with play-by-play facilitation instructions, you'll discover a roadmap for manager training that can be effective at the team, group, division, or even individual level. You will also find a variety of ready-to-use tables, tools, and worksheets to help create meaningful training experiences. The help you need to be a positive catalyst is at your fingertips.

Product order code: **110711**
ISBN-10: **1-56286-476-9**
ISBN-13: **978-1-56286-476-7**
List price: **$29.95**
Member price: $24.95

And turn the page for more great choices!

ALSO IN THIS SERIES

10 Steps to Successful Project Management

Lou Russell

Project management is a key business skill no matter your position in the organization. *10 Steps to Successful Project Management* offers you a crash course on how to ensure that your next project is delivered on time. You will learn how to distinguish between a project and a task, build a convincing business case, define the scope of the project, weigh the risks and constraints, collaborate, create a project blueprint, determine the tangible and intangible components of a project, and review lessons learned. This is a key reference for anyone wishing to improve their project management skills.

Product order code: **110705**
ISBN-10: **1-56286-463-7**
ISBN-13: **978-1-56286-463-7**
List price: **$19.95**
Member price: $17.95

10 Steps to Successful Strategic Planning

Susan Barksdale and Teri Lund

A strategic plan is central to a company's ability to make critical business decisions and develop a mission and vision that will inspire and excite employees, customers, partners, and shareholders. *10 Steps to Successful Strategic Planning* offers a simple process to help you get your organization on the path to planned success. Loaded with worksheets, exercises, tips, tools, checklists, and other easy-to-use and interactive learning aids, this book walks you through the process from beginning to end.

Product order code: **110613**
ISBN-10: **1-56286-457-2**
ISBN-13: **978-1-56286-457-6**
List price: **$19.95**
Member price: $17.95

To order, call 800.628.2783 or 703.683.8100 or visit store.astd.org